Coaching
Words of Wisdom

Quotes From The World Of Sports
To Help You Be Better
In Business and Life

Steven Howard

Caliente Press

Coaching Words of Wisdom
Quotes From the World Of Sports
To Help You Be Better In Business And Life

Published by:
Caliente Press
1775 E Palm Canyon Drive, Suite 110-198
Palm Springs, CA 92264
U.S.A.
www.CalientePress.com
Email: steven@CalientePress.com

Cover Design: Héctor Castañeda

Endorsements and Praise

In my first meeting with Steven, he helped me realize that it is all about context. Leadership is not only about leading, but on breaking through.

In a time where losing perspective and inspiration is at risk, Steven brings us a book filled with inspirational sports quotes. From the coaches who brought us great sports figures like of Serena Williams, Muhammed Ali, Billie Jean King, Michael Jordan, Marie Lou Reston, Babe Ruth, Megan Rapinoe, and many more; this is a book that honors the past, present, and future legacy of coaches around the world.

Thank you Steven for bringing this to me when I needed it the most.

Sandra Corona Matus
Sr. Global Mobility Advisor
Creator and founder of GoMoX
(the only book club in the GMS/ HR industry)

These quotes are an amazing collection of historical words, powerful words, and inspiring words.

Steven has done a masterful job in organizing these quotes. He contextually relates them to business and leadership topics while using the simple, yet effective, backdrop of sports.

I use quotes every day in my classroom to help motivate my students, and I look forward to incorporating these as well.

Todd Taylor
Assistant Professor
University of Notre Dame

Any coaching conversation, be it Leadership, Business or Health, most of the time leads us to Life matters. Steven Howard has collated wealthy quotes from life-experiences by the coaches.

My velvet pouch has gone heavier with these transformational messages. I loved the approach of categorization of quotes from Leadership to Yogism, including Motivation, Success, and more. My value favorites are bundled under Leadership, Life Lessons, and Success.

"To have long-term success as a coach or in any position of leadership, you have to be obsessed in some way," by Pat Riley, resonated deeply with me!

Thank You Steven for this wonderful collection.

Suresh MJ
Career and Leadership Coach

Steven has put quite an impressive collection of quotes together that can be applied to just about any type of situation. Whether you are mining for motivational or inspirational quotes on leadership, teamwork, the pursuit of success, or life lessons, this collection is a treasure trove.

Gary Hernbroth
Chief Motivating Officer
Training for Winners

Contents

Dedication

For Teri Rowan

Honoring a friendship
now in its fifth decade.

From those awkward, innocent teenage years
to the passing of our fathers.

Never together,
yet lives shared.

Like life, basketball is messy and unpredictable.
It has its way with you,
no matter how hard you try to control it.
The trick is to experience each moment
with a clear mind and open heart.
When you do that,
the game — and life — will take care of itself.

Phil Jackson

Introduction

Words inspire. Motivate. Inform. Educate.

Great quotes prompt reflection, spark action. They often lead to new ideas, new memorable phrases, even new personal credos.

That is my goal with *Coaching Words of Wisdom*. To inspire you. To motivate you — whether you coach children's sports activities or lead workgroups in multinational corporations. You leave your mark on this world on how you help others identify and develop their talents. That, in essence, is the fundamental role of a coach. And of parents.

This book is both for people who are leaders in their professional lives and those who are sports coaches, particularly the thousands who voluntarily coach youth sports. My other goal in creating *Coaching Words of Wisdom* is to provide you with a collection of motivational, inspirational, and educational quotations to help you develop the talents of those you coach.

I believe there are many lessons for life that we can learn from the world of sports. Lessons on success, teamwork, overcoming challenges and setbacks, dealing with adversity, striving to win, coping with losing, and the importance of continuous self-development and improvement. Many of these lessons are encapsulated in the words of wisdom found throughout this book.

The quotes in *Coaching Words of* Wisdom will help you on your journey to becoming a better coach. A coach who is trusted. A coach who is admired. A coach who people look to for motivation, inspiration, and direction. A coach destined for a rewarding and fulfilling career and life.

To be a successful leader of people, you must employ the skills of coaching. To be a successful coach, you must employ the skills of great leadership. Coaching is one of the foundational aspects of being a great leader. Great leaders are great coaches. That is why proven, best-practice coaching skills are a critical focus of emphasis in my leadership development and education programs and my leadership coaching practice.

Hopefully, *Coaching Words of Wisdom* will be my contribution to helping you identify and develop your coaching talents.

Please enjoy this collection of quotes from a vast array of coaches, Olympians, and professional athletes. And I hope you find many nuggets of inspiration and motivation – for both yourself and those you coach.

Best wishes for continued success,
Steven Howard
January 2021

CHAPTER 1

Leadership

L eadership has evolved over the years.

I believe great leadership is an art. It is the art of achieving progress through the involvement and actions of others.

This is why great leaders are strong in both leading people and leading for results, while good leaders typically focus their leadership on only one or the other.

Great leaders perform this art by applying the skills of adaptability, motivation, coaching, focus, collaboration, decision-making, communications, and personal development to both themselves and the people they lead. They also leverage the emotions of passion, enthusiasm, self-satisfaction, trust, and loyalty to drive creativity, thinking, innovation, energy, and buy-in.

Here are five other things I believe about great leadership:

> Leadership is about both people and results. If you have to neglect one, neglect the short-term results for the long-term results will come when you have developed your people.

> Great leaders are great listeners. Great leaders know they learn more from listening than from speaking. It's why you have two

ears and one mouth!

Great leaders are found at all levels of an organization. Great leadership is not confined to the executive suites or ownership ranks. You CAN become a great leader!

People development is your #1 priority. Developing your people is the single most important long-term priority and responsibility of all leaders at all levels of organizations. Great leaders ensure this happens.

Great leaders are great coaches.

There are four core aspects of being a great leader:

- Leading people
- Leading people development
- Leading for results
- Leading your own personal development and growth

Great leaders are highly skilled in eight critical areas:

- Motivating others and motiving one's self
- Communicating a clear line of value to each team member
- Prioritizing
- Leading people through change
- Setting and communicating goals
- Delegating
- Coaching
- Mindful decision making

Great leaders know that, in the words of Vice Admiral Grace Murray Hopper, "*you manage things, you lead people.*"

The quotations in this section will spark ideas on how you can better lead people.

Here's my favorite quote from these words of wisdom on leadership:

You earn your leadership every day.

Michael Jordan

Quotes on Leadership

The strength of the group is the strength of the leaders.
Vince Lombardi

Leadership is a matter of having people look at you and gain confidence, seeing how you react. If you're in control, they're in control.
Tom Landry

It is amazing how much can be accomplished if no one cares who gets the credit.
John Wooden

To have long-term success as a coach or in any position of leadership, you have to be obsessed in some way.
Pat Riley

Every leader needs to remember that a healthy respect for authority takes time to develop. It's like building trust. You don't instantly have trust; it has to be earned.
Mike Krzyzewski

Do you understand if you're going to lead, you're going to serve?
John Calipari

Earn your leadership every day.
Michael Jordan

The most important thing is to try and inspire people so that they can be great in whatever they want to do.
Kobe Bryant

There is no such thing as self-respect without respect for others.
Pat Summitt

I always mean what I say, but I don't always say what I'm thinking.
Dean Smith

If I make a mistake, I am going to make it aggressively and I am going to make it quickly. I don't believe in sleeping on the job.
Bo Schembechler

I am not remotely interested in just being good.
Vince Lombardi

People want to believe you are sincerely interested in them as a person. Not just for what they can do for you.
John Wooden

If you are going to be a leader, you're not going to please everybody. You got to hold people accountable, even if you have that moment of being uncomfortable.
Kobe Bryant

If I'm not leading by example, then I'm not doing the right thing. And I want to always do the right thing.
Pat Summitt

People are not going to follow you as a leader unless you show them that you're real. They are not going to believe you unless they trust you. And they are not going to trust you unless you always tell them the truth and admit when you are wrong.
Mike Krzyzewski

The standards you establish for others must reflect the standards you set for yourself. No one will follow a hypocrite.
Lou Holtz

Leaders have to work harder than the people they hope to motivate.
Bill Parcells

You don't lead by lip service, you lead by example.
Jim Leyland

The difference between good players and great players is that great players make others around them better.
Red Holzman

Institutions serve people, not the other way around. So as a servant-leader, I measure my success by the success of those whom I'm serving.
John Calipari

If you are a great player, every payer on that unit plays better when you are on the field.
Nick Saban

One must not hesitate to innovate and change with the times. The leader who stands still is not progressing, and he will not remain a leader for long.
Vince Lombardi

A leader must be what he wants the team to become.
John Wooden

When I gave up me, I became more. I became a captain, a leader, a better person, and I came to understand that life is a team game.
Don Mattingly

True leaders stand up to be counted in crunch time. Rather than run from the heat of a demanding job or tough judgment, they welcome it; they understand that it comes with the territory.
Bill Parcells

The topic of leadership is a touchy one. A lot of leaders fail because they don't have the bravery to touch that nerve or strike that chord. Throughout my years, I haven't had that fear.
Kobe Bryant

During critical periods, a leader is not allowed to feel sorry for himself, to be down, to be angry, or to be weak. Leaders must beat back these emotions.
Mike Krzyzewski

A leader's most powerful ally is his or her own example.
John Wooden

Leadership is getting someone to do what they don't want to do but to achieve what they want to achieve.
Tom Landry

If the leader doesn't demand it, then certainly everyone else won't expect it.
Nick Saban

For a player the responsibility of leadership cannot be turned on and off. Your ability to play well may fluctuate but your leadership cannot.
Tom Crean

The most important thing is to try and inspire people so that they can be great in whatever they want to do.
Kobe Bryant

Seek opportunities to show you care. The smallest gestures often make the biggest difference.
John Wooden

In the absence of feedback, people will fill in the blanks with a negative. They will assume you don't like them.
Pat Summitt

Listen if you want to be heard.
John Wooden

As a leader, how do you get the most out of people? Give your most to them. People notice giving and taking. Leaders give!
Kevin Eastman

Attitude affects leadership.
Joe Moorhead

I don't look at myself as a basketball coach. I look at myself as a leader who happens to coach basketball.
Mike Krzyzewski

I don't think you have to have a 'C' on your chest to be a leader. It evolves in the clubhouse.
Joe Girardi

If you're a leader, people's lives should be better because of the influence you've had along the way.
Tony Dungy

Your example isn't the main thing — it's the only thing.
Don Meyer

A leader must accomplish the difficult task of getting those on the team to believe that WE supersedes ME.
John Wooden

Moody players can cast a dark cloud over a practice and a program. The leaders of a team can NEVER accept that. Be consistent and positive!
Brittney Ezell

It is essential to understand that battles are primarily won in the hearts of men. Men respond to leadership in a most remarkable way and once you have won his heart, he will follow you anywhere.
Vince Lombardi

To be a good leader, you have to want the other guys to have success. You have to want to win more than you want to shine yourself.
John Stockton

I'm not interested in what should be, could be, was. I'm interested in what is, what we control.
Nick Saban

Leadership is getting players to believe in you. If you tell a teammate you're ready to play as tough as you're able to, you'd better go out there and do it. Players will see right through a phony. And they can tell when you're not giving it all you've got.
Larry Bird

If you want to be a leader, the first person you have to lead is yourself.
Mike Scioscia

The worst thing you can do for someone is to do something for them they can and should do for themselves.
John Wooden

Use your success, wealth and influence to put them in the best position to realize their own dreams and find their true purpose. Put them through school, set them up with job interviews and help them become leaders in their own right. Hold them to the same level of hard work and dedication that it took for you to get to where you are now, and where you will eventually go.
Kobe Bryant

Leaders are made, and they are made by effort and hard work.
Vince Lombardi

I don't know any other way to lead but by example.
Don Shula

A leader's responsibility to his team is paramount. It overshadows even his own personal feelings at any given time.
Mike Krzyzewski

If you're not loyal to your team, you can get by for a while, but eventually you will need to rely on their loyalty to you, and it just won't be there.
Tim Schafer

One thing I've learned as a coach is that you can't force your will on people. If you want them to act differently, you need to inspire them to change themselves.
Phil Jackson

It's not what you tell them, it's what they hear that matters.
Red Auerbach

Give players the opportunity to achieve without fear of failure. A pat on the back is more important than a kick in the pants.
John Wooden

You can pick captains, but you can't pick leaders. Whoever controls the locker room controls the team.
Don Meyer

People tend to look too much at numbers and not enough at where those numbers come from.
Dean Smith

Contrary to the opinion of many people, leaders are not born. Leaders are made, and they are made by effort and hard work.
Vince Lombardi

CHAPTER 2

Coaching

C oaches are more than teachers or educators.

Coaching is more than giving instructions and directions. Coaching is more about motivation, confidence-building and interactive dialogs; not prescriptive one-way directives.

Your role as a coach is to:

- Point people in the right direction
- Help people develop specific skills
- Create a team environment
- Focus on learning and improvement over winning
- Teach life skills – not just technical skills
- Build confidence as well as competency in the people you coach

Learning is necessary for growth – for the growth of individuals and for the growth of teams and organizations. The best learning comes not from being taught, but from being inspired. That is why I would rather inspire a hundred that each a thousand.

Coaching is defined by the International Federation of Coaching as "partnering with individuals in a thought-provoking and creative process that inspires them to maximize their personal and professional potential." As such, it is an on-going process, not a one-time discussion or demonstration.

To me, the key word in this definition is "partnering." Our job as coaches is to partner with the other person to help them improve specific performance and enhance the quality of their life. Our role is sometimes to give advice and direction. But more often, our role is to ask the right questions, present options, and point our coaches to finding their own solutions.

What makes a good coach? Listening is at the top of the list. Good coaches are good listeners. Great coaches are great listeners. Good coaches also have excellent empathy skills and give forthright, open, and valuable feedback. Additionally, the chemistry between both parties is also important for the coaching relationship to work effectively, especially when there is no other relationship factor (such as manager, sports coach, or parent).

A great coach is one who inspires the other person into both reflection and action. A great coach prompts and provokes an individual to a higher level of thinking and success. Thus, great coaches have an innate ability to use influence skills effectively without being coercive or manipulative.

I also believe that great coaches have a passion for helping others, combined with humbleness and not seeking credit for the improvements made and the results achieved by those they coach.

Great coaches are master motivators and solid accountability partners. They are not overly tolerant of excuses. That's because great coaches truly care for the development, growth, and success of the people they are coaching.

As you can see, there are many roles in being a coach and many skills you have to utilize.

My favorite quote from these words of wisdom on coaching is:

Coaching is unlocking a person's potential
to maximize their own performance.
It is helping them to learn rather than
teaching them.

Timothy Gallwey

Quotes on Coaching

When you want to win a game, you have to teach. When you lose a game, you have to learn.
Tom Landry

It's not my job to motivate players. They bring extraordinary motivation to our program. It's my job not to de-motivate them.
Lou Holtz

A coach's primary function should be not to make better players, but to make better people.
John Wooden

You start to realize that the trophy brings you nothing of real value. Nothing, really. The joy in coaching is helping a group of kids accomplish something they couldn't accomplish by themselves.
Billy Donovan

If you're a coach who truly respects the profession, you have to allow yourself to be coached.
John Calipari

I'm still waiting for perfection. In the meantime, I'll settle for persistence.
Bo Ryan

If you make every game a life and death proposition, you're going to have problems. For one thing, you'll be dead a lot.
Dean Smith

A life of frustration is inevitable for any coach whose main enjoyment is winning.
Chuck Noll

The only way I'd worry about the weather is if it snows on our side of the field and not theirs.
Tommy Lasorda

Players should want coaches to be hard on them. One way to tell a great player: how they react to being pushed.
Steve Nash

A man who gives you less than what he has to give is telling you what he thinks of you, and telling you what he thinks of himself.
Pete Carroll

Most people get excited about games, but I've got to be excited about practice, because that's my classroom.
Pat Summit

If I stop pushing you, if I stop demanding of you, if I stop getting on you, then I probably don't think you have much to offer.
Jon Gruden

Players think: play me and I'll show you. Coaches think: show me and I'll play you.
Shaka Smart

People aren't very good listeners, by nature. Part of being a good communicator is recognizing and understanding that and trying to make the complex simple. I try to capture a concept, an idea or a moment in a few words. If they remember it, job done.
Mike Tomlin

We would never allow for anything but full speed and full effort in games, and I wanted us to practice exactly like we played.
Peter Carroll

It doesn't matter where you coach, it matters why you coach.
Don Meyer

I do believe in praising that which deserves to be praised.
Dean Smith

If you have something critical to say to a player, preface it by saying something positive. That way when you get to the criticism, at least you know he'll be listening.
Bud Grant

The challenge is to develop the right kind of coach-player relationship so they know our intent is to get them better, and get the team better.
Steve Clifford

Coaching is unlocking a person's potential to maximize their own performance. It is helping them to learn rather than teaching them.
Timothy Gallwey

Lesson No. 1 in coaching: Don't ever assume they've got it.
Mark Richt

Discipline of others isn't punishment. You discipline to help, to improve, to correct, to prevent, not to punish, humiliate, or retaliate.
John Wooden

If we stand still, we're going backwards. We've got to keep moving forward and appear to be moving forward.
Phil Brown

If a player needed me to light a fire under him by turning the other team into a demon, he was lacking something I couldn't give him.
Bill Walsh

You must be sure to give back something that's beneficial to the game. The teaching you do must be for the benefit of those who play.
Hank Iba

They won't let you coach them up until they trust you.
Clint Hurdle

Everyone teaches you something. You listen to everyone, and bit by bit, you figure things out.
Bill Belichick

You have to coach toughness, the effort and discipline it takes to be excellent; every bit as much, if not more so than x's and o's or strategy.
Jon Gruden

You should never be proud of doing the right thing. You should just do it.
Dean Smith

Our job as a coaching staff is to show you what to do and how to do it. Your job as players is to do it consistently.
Chuck Noll

Always reward effort and good things will follow.
George Veves

Coaching needs to be less "here's what you're doing wrong" and more "here's what you need to do right."
George Raveling

Coaching is an every day event. Not something we do just at practice or game days or in season. It is all year.
Bo Schembechler

You can do more good by being good than any other way.
John Wooden

The greatest sin a coach can commit is to allow kids to slide by. This goes for the classroom as well as the court.
Hubie Brown

Every day we are going to fight lazy and soft. It's completely unacceptable. You have to be demanding.
George Karl

One of the hardest jobs in coaching is keeping the role players from undermining team chemistry.
Phil Jackson

Young people want you to be real with them.
Magic Johnson

You must invest in each person and you do so based on not their needs for attention or their needs for coaching...more so that they understand that you're trying to figure out their role in the organization and their role to help the team be successful.
Brad Stevens

If you're afraid to coach your best player, then you're not coaching anybody.
John Calipari

When you're the head coach, you're the 24/7 coach. No matter what happens, it's on your watch, and to a degree, it's your problem.
Bill Belichick

I wouldn't want to coach at some place where they didn't have high expectations for what they thought you could accomplish.
Nick Saban

You can have discipline and be demanding without being demeaning.
Don Meyer

There is a point in every contest when sitting on the sidelines is not an option.
Dean Smith

Before you can win a game, you have to not lose it.
Chuck Noll

Really, coaching is simplicity. It's getting players to play better than they think that they can.
Tom Landry

You can't pick and choose the days you feel like being responsible. It's not something that disappears when you're tired.
Pat Summitt

Even when you win, you should study what you could have done better and plan how to improve next time.
Nick Saban

A winning attitude sets consistent standards of excellence.
Mike Krzyzewski

It's hard to last in this profession if you didn't get in it for the kids.
Gary Patterson

I motivate players through communication, being honest with them, having them respect and appreciate your ability and your help.
Tommy Lasorda

If you see players who hate practice, their coach isn't doing a very good job.
Bill Walsh

I'm not here to make you feel good about bad play. I'm here to get you to understand how good you can be.
John Calipari

The pessimistic coach complains about the play. The optimistic coach expects it to change. The realistic coach adjusts what he can control.
John Kessel

Our job as coaches is to meet them where they are and not where we think they should be.
Tom Kelsey

You can't coach everyone the same way. Ask yourself: how can I reach him?
Nick Saban

So often we fail to acknowledge what we have because we're so concerned about what we want.
John Wooden

In order to grow, you must accept new responsibilities, no matter how uncertain you may feel or how unprepared you are to deal with them.
Pat Summitt

Integrity doesn't come in degrees: low, medium, or high. You either have integrity or you don't.
Tony Dungy

Your number one job as a coach is to make your players better men in society. If they become better players that's a bonus.
Charles Barkley

I won't quit on a player who doesn't quit on himself.
Charlie Manuel

Perhaps the toughest call for a coach is weighing what is best for an individual against what is best for the team.
Tom Landry

You can never pay back, so you should always try to pay forward.
Woody Hayes

Coaches who make excuses shouldn't be surprised when their players start to offer them too.
Gary Curneen

Part of coaching is acting. It's true of any kind of leadership, whether you're a CEO, an army general, or a father. Part of the job is that you don't reveal your own apprehensions.
John Calipari

It's what you learn after you know it all that counts.
John Wooden

Players respond to coaches who really have their best interests at heart.
Mike Singletary

The greatest thing I've got going for me is my ability to believe in other people's talents. I can see people doing things they can't see themselves doing.
Bob Rotella

Discipline is the greatest form of love you can show someone. Great players crave discipline.
Tom Izzo

A coach is someone who tells you what you don't want to hear, who has you see what you don't want to see, so you can be who you have always known you could be.
Tom Landry

As coaches we must encourage weakness by applauding players when they fail for the right reasons.
Johan Cruyff

They call it coaching, but it's teaching. You do not just tell them — you show them the reasons.
Vince Lombardi

More than winning, I believe it is our job as coaches to develop our players into responsible leaders.
Pat Summitt

You can only really yell at the players you trust.
Bill Parcells

Praise the actions you want repeated.
Dean Smith

You need to have a plan for the worst scenario. It doesn't mean that it will always work, but you will always be prepared.
Bill Walsh

Just because guys have big personalities doesn't mean they're hard to manage. As a manager, your obligation is to try to communicate with everybody on the team — not just young, or old, or quiet, or loud — everybody.
Terry Francona

Sometimes you will hate me because I will tell you the truth about your game. And the truth can hurt or humble you.
Doc Rivers

While you can't control what happens to you, you can control how you react.
John Wooden

Coaching is not what you know, but what you can get your players to do on the court.
Stan Van Gundy

Get the kids to understand that they shouldn't worry about who makes the shot, only whether or not the shot is made.
Pete Carroll

There are so many ways to play this game; we must never forget that the one constant is relationships.
Sue Gunter

No coach has ever won a game by what he knows; it's what his players know that counts.
Paul (Bear) Bryant

Habits are critical for players. They cannot think and play well at the same time.
Don Meyer

I enjoy winning and very much dislike losing — but I did not allow either of them to obsess me. I was a silent loser, believing that if you won you said little, and if you lost you said even less.
Paul Brown

We try to recruit character. No one has perfect character. My philosophy in coaching is if you recruit character, you can challenge it. If you challenge someone with no character, they will quit on you. If you challenge people with character, they will come back and fight.
Jim Molinari

You have to have a contingency plan for adversity because you're gonna face it. Period. You only choice is how you respond to it.
Jon Gruden

I've always tried to coach people the way I would like to be coached; positively and encouragingly rather than with criticism and fear. I've tried to be as fair as possible.
Tony Dungy

Keep it simple. I'm not interested in trying to prove to my players that I'm a genius.
John Thompson

Value those colleagues who tell you the truth, not just what you want to hear.
Pat Summitt

90% of coaching is creating an environment, through force of personality. The other 10% involves strategy.
Steve Kerr

Give role players love. Praise can be most valuable when it's merited by someone whose supporting role is often overlooked.
Bill Parcells

I love practice. It is when a coach exercises the most control over the improvement of his or her team.
Mike Krzyzewski

I think every coach in America would benefit from coaching at a school that's the underdog most of the time.
Steve Spurrier

You should pay more attention to how they learn than you do to how you teach.
Pat Kirwan

The best competition I have is against myself to become better.
John Wooden

I think that there are a lot of things you can't change, that are out of your control, but your attitude is in your control.
Scotty Bowman

Whatever success I've had it is because I've tried to understand the situation of the player. I think the coach's duty is to avoid complicating matters.
Bill Belichick

You can't always control circumstances — you can always control your attitude, approach, and response.
Tony Dungy

If a player makes what looks like a poor decision, confront it, but in the right way. Ask, "Tell me what you saw" and listen.
Clint Hurdle

If a man is a quitter, I'd rather find out in practice than in a game. I ask for all a player has so I'll know later what I can expect.
Paul (Bear) Bryant

Nine-tenths of discipline is having the patience to do things right.
Pat Summitt

Discipline is not a light switch. Discipline is a way of life.
John Harbaugh

The only correct actions are those that demand no explanation and no apology.
Red Auerbach

I'd never get away with what I do if the players feel I didn't care for them. They know, in the long run, I'm in their corner.
Bo Schembechler

Each group and each youngster is different. As a leader or coach, you get to know what they need.
Mike Krzyzewski

You can never let off the gas. You have to keep going and pursuing being the best you can every day.
Brad Stevens

Sometimes the best way to help a player is to simply encourage them rather than give them an abundance of information.
Gary Curneen

Good coaching is about leadership and instilling respect in your players. Dictators lead through fear — good coaches do not.
John Wooden

How competitive can you be without losing your discipline?
Doc Rivers

You should always want your coach to be critical. It gives you an opportunity to learn and to overcome adversity.
Steve Nash

I'm no miracle man. I guarantee nothing but hard work.
Paul (Bear) Bryant

Holding people accountable to high standards is nothing to apologize for. Failing to stretch them to their potential is.
Dave Anderson

I believe strongly that there's a better way to motivate than through intimidation.
Dick Vermeil

A coach who allows players to depart from his plan at practice can expect the same thing in a game.
Dr. Jack Ramsay

It's not about talent, it's about heart. It's about who can go out there and play the hardest. They're not going to give us anything, so you've got to go out there and you've got to take it.
Don Haskins

If we fail to adapt, we fail to move forward.
John Wooden

Your decisions reveal your priorities.
Jeff Van Gundy

The single most important aspect of coaching is running effective practices.
Bob Knight

The definition of discipline is to do what you're supposed to do when you're supposed to do it.
Jim Larrañaga

You can't force your will on people. If you want them to act differently, you need to inspire them to change themselves.
Phil Jackson

I've been around young, talented, noncoachable players. I've been around veteran, talented, noncoachable players. No matter what you do, sooner or later even if a coach comes in that's able to connect with them, if that's who they are, they're going to go back to it.
Scott Brooks

Building relationships is the key for being happy as a coach. Players must want to play for you. If they are comfortable with you, they will work hard for you.
Mike McConathy

Mental toughness is doing the right thing for the team when it's not the best thing for you.
Bill Belichick

If I'm honest with you, you might not like me for a day or two. But if I lie to you, you're going to hate me forever.
Joe Maddon

Here's how I'm going to beat you. I'm going to outwork you. That's it. That's all there is to it.
Pat Summitt

If something bad happens we can't multiply it by dropping our heads.
Avery Johnson

My door is always open to talk about playing time. If you want to talk about playing time, be prepared for the truth.
Brad Stevens

You don't win games as a coach during games. You win games as a coach before games. Players win during games, not coaches.
Red Auerbach

A coach tells you what you don't want to hear, has you see what you don't want to see, so you can be who you have always known you could be.
Tom Landry

Let me give so much time to the improvement of myself that I shall have no time to criticize others.
John Wooden

It is foolish to expect a young man to follow your advice and ignore your example.
Don Meyer

Discipline is not punishment. Discipline is changing someone's behavior.
Nick Saban

If we don't force players to react to things, put them in tough situations, then it's our fault they can't react to them in games.
Bobby Knight

If you're going to have to beg them to play, it's not going to work.
Chuck Daly

If you want people to be flexible, adaptable and open to feedback, so must you.
George Raveling

You have to establish a winning mentality. We want to be demanding of guys. We're not out there just playing some pickup game.
Jeff Hornacek

A little negative thing must be dealt with immediately — before it becomes a big negative thing.
Mike Krzyzewski

Don't focus all of our attention on what we want, focus on who we are.
Brad Stevens

All coaches have a powerful ally, but most are afraid to use it — the bench.
John Wooden

Take care of the tiniest detail, because the little details add up until they represent significant differences. Let nothing slip through the cracks.
Bill Belichick

For us, the thing that works best is total, brutal, between-the-eyes honesty. I never try to trick a player or manipulate them, tell them something that I'm going to have to change next week.
Gregg Popovich

Coaches win practices, players win games.
Pete Carroll

Best training environments are built on standards — what's acceptable and what isn't. You cannot disrupt mediocrity if you cannot identify it.
Gary Curneen

Eliminate the clutter and all the things that are going on outside and focus on the things that you can control with how you go about and take care of your business. That's something that's ongoing, and it can never change.
Nick Saban

You discipline those under your supervision to correct, to help, and to improve. Not to punish.
John Wooden

A common mistake among those who work in sport is spending a disproportional amount of time on "x's and o's," as compared to time spent learning about people.
Mike Krzyzewski

What excites me is finding a kid who doesn't even know how good he can be, and helping him realize that potential. That's the joy of coaching.
Jamie Dixon

The more successful you are, the more responsibility you must assume.
Pat Summitt

If you want to be a winner you practice the right way. I saw the wrong way being practiced and I said something.
David Ross

First you coach the man, then you coach the player.
Babe Laufenberg

You can run a lot of plays when your X is twice as big as the other guy's O. It makes your X's and O's pretty good.
Paul Westphal

I figured this was the easy stuff, and if we couldn't show up on time, looking right and acting right, we weren't going to be able to do anything else.
Bo Schembechler

The best thing any coach at any level can do for their player is hold them accountable.
Jeff Boals

Before correcting a player, first tell them one thing they are doing well and why. Then tell them one thing WE can be doing better.
Don Meyer

Once you have done everything that you possibly can —
you've put forth your greatest effort — then I can live with
whatever's next.
Bill Parcells

A big part of coaching is the human element, getting guys
to buy in, to play together, to accept roles, and put them in
the right system.
Gar Forman

I think you have to be what you are. Don't try to be
somebody else. You have to be yourself at all times.
John Wooden

Coaching is by far the best profession you could ever be in
— you have the chance to be significant.
Lou Holtz

Coaching is unlocking a person's potential to maximize
their own performance. It is helping them to learn rather
than teaching them.
Timothy Gallwey

You can't stand up in front of the team and point the finger
all day at the players. You're in it together.
Bill O'Brien

Anytime you are trying to bring out the best in someone,
there is going to be creative tension.
Doug Collins

I don't treat my players equally. I treat them fairly.
Pat Summitt

Praise is a great motivator. Criticism is a great teaching tool if done properly, but praise is the best motivator.
John Wooden

Sometimes it's easier to criticize than to praise. Winning coaches look for opportunities to praise.
Bill Parcells

We control by attitudes, positive mental attitudes, not by rules.
Woody Hayes

Don't take anything for granted. Nothing in life gets better by accident.
Dick Vermeil

If you don't want responsibility, don't sit in the big chair. That's the deal. To be successful, you must accept full responsibility. Even when it doesn't seem fair.
Pat Summitt

'Coach' is one of the greatest titles anybody can have. They impact kids' lives in a way that no other teacher does.
Phil Knight

CHAPTER 3

Building Winning Teams

Creating and maintaining a high-performing team is rarely a natural occurrence. It takes considered effort and thinking to craft a cohesive, collaborating collective of individuals who will be supportive and appreciative of one another.

One of my core beliefs is that leadership is about both people and results. If you have to neglect one, neglect the short-term results for the long-term results will come when you have developed your people. After all, that is what building a winning team is all about – a team that can win for the long-term.

In fact, the key judging criteria for evaluating a team's long-term success is straight-forward: can this group work cohesively together on another project or next season?

When the focus is on short-term results, you may not have a team capable of working together effectively over the long term. You may get the results you want, or win the championship, but underlying tension and friction may prevent future successes.

Psychologist Bruce Tuckman gave us a great model for building winning teams that leaders and coaches seem to overlook these days. In 1965, Tuckman defined the four stages of group development as forming, storming, norming, and performing. A reminder: just because something is a 55-year-old model does not mean it has zero relevance today.

Great leaders know that performance results are best derived by the engagement and motivation of team members, particularly those who receive continuous skill development. Organizational energy, workplace synergy, and results are best attained when motivated people with different backgrounds and thinking preferences are allowed to work together safely and in a supportive environment.

Great leaders create such successful and supportive climates by applying the skills of adaptability, motivation, coaching, focus, collaboration, mindful decision-making, open and transparent communications, and skill development of both themselves and the people they lead.

Winning teams in the workplace – and the world of sports – are created by coaches who focus on four critical areas to increase engagement and drive results:

1. Giving team members a sense of purpose and a compelling context for commitment and buy-in.

2. Granting team members appropriate levels of autonomy.

3. Showing empathy to team members by understanding the emotions and feelings they are going through, particularly during tough or uncertain times.

4. Creating a safe environment where mistakes

are tolerated and learned from, and accountability is fair and unbiased.

That last point is critical. Let people learn from mistakes and errors. If someone makes a mistake and learns something, then it is no longer a mistake.

Additionally, hold each other accountable. Not just for results or following procedures. Everyone in the team should hold each other accountable for the decisions and options producing the results, as well as for the actual outcomes. Additionally, accountability is not just about owning up to mistakes. Accountability means being true to the purpose and values that drive your organization, business unit, or team.

Winning teams are built on a foundation of trust. Trust and respect among team members, and between the team leader and team members, is critical. If trust is absent, collaboration and working partnerships will not happen. Your trust as a leader and a coach must be built on transparency, authenticity, credibility, accountability, and flexibility.

My favorite quote from these words of wisdom on building winning teams is:

> *On good teams, coaches hold players accountable;*
> *on great teams, players hold players accountable.*

Joe Dumars

Quotes on Building Winning Teams

Sometimes a player's greatest challenge is coming to grips with his role on the team.
Scottie Pippen

A player who makes a team great is much more valuable than a great player.
John Wooden

Love is the force that ignites the spirit and binds teams together.
Phil Jackson

A team will always appreciate a great individual if he's willing to sacrifice for the group.
Kareem Abdul-Jabbar

Winning as a team is better than anything. It's great to share success.
Jim Harbaugh

The most difficult thing for individuals to do when they're part of the team is to sacrifice. Without sacrifice you'll never know your team's potential.
Pat Riley

Communication does not always occur naturally, even among a tight-knit group of individuals. Communication must be taught and practiced in order to bring everyone together as one.
Mike Krzyzewski

I haven't always recruited for the best talent. I've taken a few guys who would fit for different reasons — leadership, toughness.
Tom Izzo

These guys have been through a lot. They've seen the good runs. They've seen the bad runs. But this group never gets discouraged to the point where they get down on themselves or their teammates, and that's what's fun.
Bo Ryan

Basketball is a team game but that doesn't mean all five players should have the same amount of shots.
Dean Smith

Teamwork is what the Green Bay Packers were all about. They didn't do it for individual glory. They did it because they loved one another.
Vince Lombardi

A team is where a boy can prove his courage on his own. A gang is where a coward goes to hide.
Mickey Mantle

Don't let winning make you soft. Don't let losing make you quit. Don't let your teammates down in any situation.
Larry Bird

The main ingredient of stardom is the rest of the team.
John Wooden

Your best players have to unite and inspire the group. Otherwise, they'll divide the group.
Jeff Van Gundy

Responsibility equals accountability equals ownership. And a sense of ownership is the most powerful weapon a team or organization can have.
Pat Summitt

On good teams coaches hold players accountable, on great teams players hold players accountable.
Joe Dumars

The achievements of an organization are the results of the combined effort of each individual.
Vince Lombardi

Everybody has to bring his "A" game. The combination of individuals being able to do that is what creates the identity of the team.
Nick Saban

In sports, teams win and individuals don't.
Fran Tarkenton

On a team, it's not the strength of the individual players, but it is the strength of the unit and how they all function together.
Bill Cleveland

If you are going to have a great team, there should be no excuses and no finger-pointing when somebody else is not perfect.
Mike Krzyzewski

Sometimes you get these individuals where that's all they want to do: when the team's got the ball, I'll play, but when we haven't got the ball I'll go and have a rest.
George Graham

I recruit hungry kids, kids that love the game and want to get better and feel they have more questions than answers. It is very hard to find, but we've got 'em,
Bo Ryan

It's been great that guys have bought into something, and I think that's what they've bought into, the team concept of defense, helping one another, knowing they're not good enough individually, but collectively, they've done an incredible job.
Tom Izzo

If you can't accept someone getting on you when you're wrong, then you're not about the team.
Raymond Felton

You need to work as hard to be a great teammate as you do to be a great player.
Jon Gruden

Everybody likes each other until things get tough. Then you find out what kind of team you have.
Doc Rivers

I just think every time you go through one of those tests, your team gets closer. They start believing and trusting more.
Doc Rivers

The game is easy if you do it the right way and you play with a great effort and you play together as a team.
Scott Brooks

To build a powerful team, you must be willing to be surrounded by people who are better than you are in some areas.
Stephen Mansfield

Our job isn't to assemble the best players, it's to put together the best team.
Bill Belichick

I think everybody should take the attitude that we're working to be a champion, that we want to be a champion in everything that we do. Every choice, every decision, everything that we do every day, we want to be a champion.
Nick Saban

To get a group of highly competitive people to play roles and sacrifice for the team for the greater good is really hard, which is why it isn't done very often.
Steve Kerr

The measure of who we are is how we react to something that doesn't go our way.
Gregg Popovich

The first thing you do is weed out selfishness. No program can be successful with players who put themselves ahead of the team.
Johnny Majors

A team in an ordinary frame of mind will do ordinary things. In the proper emotional state, a team will do extraordinary things. To reach this state, a team must have a motive that has an extraordinary appeal to them.
Knute Rockne

I have a rule on my team: When we talk to one another, we look each other right in the eye, because I think it's tough to lie to somebody. You give respect to somebody.
Mike Krzyzewski

We cannot have two standards, one set for the dedicated players who want to do something ambitious and one set for those who don't.
Paul (Bear) Bryant

You have to have players who buy into your system, demand the best from themselves and their teammates, and hold teammates accountable.
Pat Summitt

In championship cultures, teammates hold each other accountable to championship attitudes and actions.
Jeff Janssen

Part of cultivating a productive culture is having fun together. Teams are more successful when they do.
Hayden Fry

No one is bigger than the team. You're going to be on time, you're going to play hard, you're going to know your job and you're going to know when to pass and shoot. If you can't do those four things, you're not getting time here.
Hubie Brown

I think teams win. I don't think offense wins. I don't think defense wins. I don't' think special teams win. Teams win.
Dabo Swinney

Players who are late are saying their time is more important than the team.
Don Meyer

One thing about championship teams is that they're resilient. No matter what is thrown at them, no matter how deep the hole, they find a way to bounce back and overcome adversity.
Nick Saban

Great players and great teams want to be driven. They want to be pushed to the edge. They don't want to be cheated. Ordinary players and average teams want it to be easy.
Pat Riley

That's what defines chemistry. Guys have roles, they respect those roles and play to the ability of those roles.
Lionel Hollins

Culture doesn't change when a coach tells a player he's wrong. It changes when players tell other players: no, that's not how we do things here.
Jeff Hecklinski

Teams that never concede defeat can accomplish incredible victories.
Dr. Jack Ramsay

You team is going to go a lot further if your stars push ahead, and everybody else has to work to catch up.
Mike Krzyzewski

When the older players are willing to help the younger players every day, then you've got the right environment to build a winner.
Hank Iba

Being part of something that is working toward a greater goal. There's no more satisfaction than achieving goals as a team.
Jim Harbaugh

Every time you skip a rep behind your coach's back you are not tricking him, you are cheating your teammates and yourself.
Senquez Golson

Even when you're getting part-time minutes, you still have full-time commitment to your teammates and coaches.
Jim Afremow

No individual can win a game by himself.
Pelé

The best players on the team believe in our culture and let us coach them.
Jay Wright

You must learn how to hold a team together. You must lift some men up, calm others down, until finally they've got one heartbeat. Then you've got yourself a team.
Paul (Bear) Bryant

Dependability is more important than ability.
Bill Belichick

Having a successful team does not mean that everyone must have the same desires and motivations. But every team member must channel those motivators toward performing at his best and doing what is best for the team.
Nick Saban

Know your role. Stay in your role. Star in your role.
Doug Collins

To me, teamwork is the beauty of our sport, where you have five acting as one. You become selfless.
Mike Krzyzewski

Great teamwork is the only way we create the breakthroughs that define our careers.
Pat Riley

The strength of the team is each individual member. The strength of each member is the team.
Phil Jackson

Ultimately, being part of a team means competing, working, living, and winning and losing together.
Steve Kerr

How your team complements each other is just as important as their individual skill sets.
Jerry Colangelo

There are a lot of commonsense advantages to running a team like a family —honesty, strength, caring, and so on. But one of the greatest strengths is the fact that, in a family, you are never alone. There are built-in allies.
Mike Krzyzewski

You can never have enough high character guys that are committed to each other.
Scott Brooks

The game itself is an autonomous game, but everybody is a part of it. No contribution is too small.
Joe Torre

Create an environment where everybody knows his or her responsibilities — and each is responsible to the entire group.
Nick Saban

Oneness is not something you can turn on with a switch. You need to create the right environment for it to grow, then nurture it carefully every day.
Phil Jackson

If you don't have accountability, you will not improve.
Brad Stevens

Every play in practice is a statement of your commitment to your teammates.
Tom Herman

You don't inspire your teammates by showing them how amazing you are. You inspire them by showing them how amazing they are.
Robyn Benincasa

We want men here, not just players. Players are a dime a dozen.
Tom Izzo

To be a good player on your team, you have to affect someone else on the team. You have to cause them to play better by the way you play.
Nick Saban

I believe God gave us crises for some reason — and it certainly wasn't for us to say that everything about them is bad. A crisis can be a momentous time for a team to grow — if a leader handles it properly.
Mike Krzyzewski

Five guys on the court working together can achieve more than five talented individuals who come and go as individuals.
Kareem Abdul-Jabbar

Defense brings teams together. Offense makes teams feel good, but the defense is what brings teams together.
Doc Rivers

If players never pick up another teammate during a tough session, they're saying, "I am only concerned about myself right now."
Gary Curneen

There's nothing greater in the world than when somebody on the team does something good and everybody gathers around to pat him on the back.
Billy Martin

I'd take a 2-star recruit with a 5-star work ethic over a 5-star recruit with a 2-star work ethic any day.
Mike Krzyzewski

Individual commitment to a group effort — that is what makes a team work.
Vince Lombardi

If you're going to have a team of role players, you'd better have a team of guys who truly understand their roles.
Steve Kerr

We don't have to be superstars or win championships. All we have to do is learn to rise to every occasion, give our best effort, and make those around us better as we do it.
John Wooden

What you want guys to do when there's adversity is to play harder and play better, and that's when you see what kind of guys you have in your locker room.
Mike Shanahan

How good can we expect to be if our best player is not our best teammate?
Brad Stevens

If you care about winning, you talk to your teammates.
Frank Martin

Teams that play together beat those teams with superior players who play more as individuals.
Dr. Jack Ramsay

Think what a great thing it is to be part of something that is THE TEAM.
Bo Schembechler

There are three things we can't have. We can't have complacency, we can't have selfishness, and we can't lose our accountability.
Nick Saban

All it takes is one person who is committed, focused, and on a mission to spark an entire team into believing in themselves.
Bruce Brown

The winning team has a dedication. It will have a core of veteran players who set the standards. They will not accept defeat.
Merlin Olsen

You never want players who are content with staying in the same spot. The best players are the ones with a thirst to grow, the ones who are always looking for ways to improve.
Eric Musselman

The locker room, the team spirit, it's all connected. If you've got a guy who's sour, it sucks the life out of the group.
Jack Del Rio

It's all about preparation. That's how it's supposed to be done. That's how championship teams do it.
Mike Pagliarulo

Do your role as well as you possibly can and become a superstar in that role. Give it everything you got.
Brad Stevens

If your best player is your hardest worker, you've got a chance to be a good team.
Don Meyer

When the players and teammates are talking to each other on the court, that's what makes a team good.
Jeff Hornacek

Losers assemble in little groups and complain, but winners assemble as a team.
Bill Parcells

Learn to hold a team together. Lift some up, calm others down, until finally they've got one heartbeat. Then you've got a team.
Paul (Bear) Bryant

When you build the right culture, you don't have to kick people off the bus. They will get off themselves because they don't fit in.
Jon Gordon

If you play the game for your teammates and not for yourself, it becomes much easier.
John Calipari

Teamwork is the foundation of success. The three universal questions that an individual asks of his coach, player, employee, employer are: Can I trust you? Are you committed to excellence? And do you are about me?
Lou Holtz

A team is a group of players who support one another on court and who think of the group before they think of themselves.
K. C. Jones

Your best player has to set a tone of intolerance for anything that gets in the way of winning.
Jeff Van Gundy

Chemistry is not something that just happens. You have to work at it.
Bruce Bochy

You don't just be a team. You become a team. Through tough games you find that you need each other.
Mike Krzyzewski

Players who are committed to the team first will find a way to help when things are going bad, they will do whatever it takes.
Dick Bennett

Don't look at your teammates as competition. If you can make them better, you'll improve as a player and everything else will fall into place.
Patrick Patterson

There are three fights that a team has to fight every day: division from within, competition, and outside influences.
Bill Parcells

Being a good teammate is still doing your part when things are going bad for you. Being a good team is helping that player get out of it.
Kevin Eastman

The most important measure of how good a game I played was how much better I'd made my teammates play.
Bill Russell

We're going to believe in each other, not criticize each other. We're going to encourage each other, not talk about each other.
Bo Schembechler

When your best player's working harder than everybody and holding everyone accountable, that's a winning culture.
Grant Hill

Pushing and getting through the uncomfortable by yourself builds a player. Pushing someone else through uncomfortable builds a team.
Tom Crean

In order to have a winner, a team must have a feeling of unity. Every player must put the team first — ahead of personal glory.
Paul (Bear) Bryant

Play the right way means play unselfishly, respect each other's achievements, play hard, fulfill your role.
Gregg Popovich

Good teams don't care about who scores. Good teams just care about scoring; they don't care who does it.
George Karl

Culture is what we believe, how we behave, and the experience that our behavior produces for each other.
Urban Meyer

Great teams are connected to a greater purpose.
Don Yaeger

Average teammates are interested in their teammates. Great teammates are invested in their teammates.
Tom Crean

It should always be about team. You can't play everybody. But if you're not playing, you've still got to be a good teammate.
Mike Woodson

Losing yourself in the group, for the good of the group, that's teamwork.
John Wooden

Our goal is not to win. It's to play together and play hard. Then, winning takes care of itself.
Mike Krzyzewski

You have to be able to look at the man next to you as your brother. You have to become a family.
LeBron James

I always ask my teams to own their performances. That means taking responsibility for everything – the good and the bad.
John Calipari

You have to protect your team culture. This battle is waged daily.
Doc Rivers

I don't want a player that's content with not playing.
Don Shula

It's not about any one person. You've got to get over yourself and realize that it takes a group to get things done.
Gregg Popovich

It's not the most physically talented teams that win, it's the team that can best use its talents that wins.
Phil Jackson

The best teams have chemistry. They communicate with each other and they sacrifice personal glory for the common goal.
Dave DeBusschere

There are no shortcuts to building a team each season. You build the foundation brick by brick.
Bill Belichick

The team will function more effectively when it has leaders and team members who refuse to blame their teammates.
Mike Smith

Winning and championships are memorable but they come from the strength of the relationships.
Jim Calhoun

Whoever it is coming off the bench, that person has to be able to come in and lift the game.
John Calipari

There are a lot of different things that go into Chemistry on a team but it begins and ends with MUTUAL RESPECT amongst teammates.
Tom Crean

This is the bottom line: We win or lose together. Great teams embrace responsibility. It's that simple.
Mike Krzyzewski

Do you want to know who your best teammates are? Watch how they react when someone else does something good.
Phil Beckner

A shared culture will quickly show the new team member how he is expected to act. Personal agendas are not tolerated within the standards of a strong organization.
Kevin Eastman

Go with players you believe in, who fit your personality and your system.
Jimmy Johnson

Everyone on your team is important. Importance knows no rank.
Mike Krzyzewski

If your best player accepts coaching, wants you to coach him, doesn't run away from it, doesn't pout, doesn't cry, comes in the next day and he is as excited as he was the day before, it sets the tone for everyone else to fall in line and accept coaching.
Frank Martin

A team in an ordinary frame of mind will do ordinary things. In the proper emotional state, a team will do extraordinary things. To reach this state, a team must have a motive that has an extraordinary appeal to them.
Knute Rockne

The first thing you do is weed out selfishness. No program can be successful with players who put themselves ahead of the team.
Johnny Majors

Culture beats strategy. Strategy is important but it's your culture that will determine whether your strategy is successful.
Jon Gordon

Part of cultivating a productive culture is having fun together. Teams are more successful when they do.
Hayden Fry

We are no better than anyone else when they aren't ready, when they play as individuals and not as one.
Vince Lombardi

We don't have to be perfect. We just have to stay together.
Rick Barnes

Culture doesn't change when coach tells a player he's wrong. It changes when players tell other players: no that's not how we do things here.
Jeff Hecklinski

Teamwork is the only way to reach our ultimate moments, and create breakthroughs that define our careers and fulfill our lives.
Pat Riley

You cannot merely expect culture to be a natural occurrence; it has to be taught and made a part of your everyday routine.
Mike Krzyzewski

Great players and great teams want to be driven. They want to be pushed to the edge. They don't want to be cheated. Ordinary players and average teams want it to be easy.
Pat Riley

Encourage team play — achieve results through cooperation and unselfish effort on the part of every player.
Dean Smith

The culture precedes positive results. Champions behave like champions before they're champions; they have a winning standard of performance before they are winners.
Bill Walsh

Winning teams at any level all play team basketball. Championship teams have five players on the same page at all times.
Hubie Brown

The single most important ingredient after you get the talent is internal leadership. It's not the coaches as much as one single person or people on the team who set higher standards than that team would normally set itself.
Mike Krzyzewski

I'm not looking for the best players, I'm looking for the right ones.
Herb Brooks

That's when you know you really have something going, when the players are starting to hold themselves accountable.
Scott Skiles

The challenge of every team is to build a feeling of oneness, of dependence on one another because the question is usually not how well each person performs, but how well they work together.
Vince Lombardi

There are five fundamental qualities that make every team great: communication, trust, collective responsibility, caring, and pride.
Mike Krzyzewski

CHAPTER 4

The Two Greatest

Muhammed Ali and Michael Jordan.

Both dominated their respective sports. Both with larger-than-life personalities. Both highly quotable. Both motivated and inspired millions of people across the globe.

Both taught us life lessons as we vicariously watched their lives unfold.

One proclaimed himself, "The Greatest." The other was named such by the media, peers, former players, fans, and just about everyone else who saw him fly to the rim.

One was a mega force for social justice, equality, and religious freedom. The other kept relatively quiet on social issues during his playing days, though he has contributed both verbally and financially to various societal issues in recent years.

Listed below are their respective words of wisdom, which will endure for the benefit of future generations of coaches, athletes, leaders, and humanity.

Quotes From
The Two Greatest
Ali and Jordan

I know where I'm going and I know the truth, and I don't have to be what you want me to be. I'm free to be what I want.
Muhammad Ali

He who is not courageous enough to take risks will accomplish nothing in life.
Muhammad Ali

Don't count the days; make the days count.
Muhammad Ali

What you're thinking is what you're becoming.
Muhammad Ali

Service to others is the rent you pay for your room here on earth.
Muhammad Ali

Champions aren't made in gyms. Champions are made from something they have deep inside them — a desire, a dream, a vision. They have to have the skill, and the will. But the will must be stronger than the skill.
Muhammad Ali

Only a man who knows what it is like to be defeated can reach down to the bottom of his soul and come up with the extra ounce of power it takes to win when the match is even.
Muhammad Ali

If they can make penicillin out of moldy bread, they can sure make something out of you.
Muhammad Ali

I shook up the world. Me! Whee!
Muhammad Ali

It isn't the mountains ahead to climb that wear you out; it's the pebble in your shoe.
Muhammad Ali

Life is a gamble. You can get hurt, but people die in plane crashes, lose their arms and legs in car accidents; people die every day. Same with fighters: some die, some get hurt, some go on. You just don't let yourself believe it will happen to you.
Muhammad Ali

I should be a postage stamp. That's the only way I'll ever get licked.
Muhammad Ali

 Friendship is the hardest thing in the world to explain. It's not something you learn in school. But if you haven't learned the meaning of friendship, you really haven't learned anything.
Muhammad Ali

The best way to make your dreams come true is to wake up.
Muhammad Ali

You lose nothing when fighting for a cause. In my mind the losers are those who don't have a cause they care about.
Muhammad Ali

It's lack of faith that makes people afraid of meeting challenges, and I believed in myself.
Muhammad Ali

A man who views the world the same at fifty as he did at twenty has wasted thirty years of his life.
Muhammad Ali

I never thought of losing, but now that it's happened, the only thing is to do it right. That's my obligation to all the people who believe in me. We all have to take defeats in life.
Muhammad Ali

I hated every minute of training, but I said, "Don't quit. Suffer now and live the rest of your life as a champion."
Muhammed Ali

It's repetition of affirmations that leads to belief. And once that belief becomes a deep conviction, things begin to happen.
Muhammad Ali

What keeps me going is goals.
Muhammad Ali

The man who has no imagination has no wings.
Muhammad Ali

Impossible is just a big word thrown around by small men who find it easier to live in the world they've been given than to explore the power they have to change it. Impossible is not a fact. It's an opinion. Impossible is not a declaration. It's a dare. Impossible is potential. Impossible is temporary. Impossible is nothing.
Muhammad Ali

Inside of a ring or out, ain't nothing wrong with going down. It's staying down that's wrong.
Muhammad Ali

Children make you want to start life over.
Muhammad Ali

If you even dream of beating me you'd better wake up and apologize.
Muhammad Ali

I'm young, I'm handsome, I'm fast. And I can't possibly be beat.
Muhammad Ali

To be a great champion, you must believe you are the best. If you're not, pretend you are.
Muhammad Ali

If my mind can conceive it, and my heart can believe it, then I can achieve it.
Muhammad Ali

At home I am a nice guy: but I don't want the world to know. Humble people, I've found, don't get very far.
Muhammad Ali

It's hard to be humble when you're as great as I am.
Muhammad Ali

Hating people because of their color is wrong. And it doesn't matter which color does the hating. It's just plain wrong.
Muhammad Ali

It's not bragging if you can back it up.
Muhammad Ali

Live every day as if it were your last because someday you're going to be right.
Muhammad Ali

It's a lack of faith that makes people afraid of meeting challenges, and I believed in myself.
Muhammad Ali

I know where I'm going and I know the truth, and I don't have to be what you want me to be. I'm free to be what I want.
Muhammad Ali

Tolerance and understanding won't "trickle-down" in our society any more than wealth does.
Muhammad Ali

What you are thinking is what you are becoming.
Muhammad Ali

Age is whatever you think it is. You are as old as you think you are.
Muhammad Ali

I am the greatest, I said that even before I knew I was. I figured that if I said it enough, I would convince the world that I really was the greatest.
Muhammad Ali

Silence is golden when you can't think of a good answer.
Muhammad Ali

It is the repetition of affirmations that leads to belief. And once that belief becomes a deep conviction, things begin to happen.
Muhammad Ali

Float like a butterfly, sting like a bee.
Muhammad Ali

When a man says I cannot, he has made a suggestion to himself. He has weakened his power of accomplishing that which otherwise would have been accomplished.
Muhammad Ali

Rivers, ponds, lakes and streams – they all have different names, but they all contain water. Just as religions do – they all contain truths.
Muhammad Ali

I never thought of losing, but now that it's happened, the only thing is to do it right. That's my obligation to all the people who believe in me. We all have to take defeats in life.
Muhammad Ali

I wish people would love everybody else the way they love me. It would be a better world.
Muhammad Ali

You're my opposer when I want freedom; you're my opposer when I want justice; you're my opposer when I want equality. You won't even stand up for me in America for my religious beliefs and you want me to go somewhere and fight. But you won't even stand up for me here at home!
Muhammad Ali

To be able to give away riches is mandatory if you wish to possess them. This is the only way that you will be truly rich.
Muhammad Ali

Friendship is a priceless gift that cannot be bought nor sold, but its value is far greater than a mountain made of gold.
Muhammad Ali

I am a Muslim and there is nothing Islamic about killing innocent people in Paris, San Bernardino, or anywhere else in the world.
Muhammad Ali

Wisdom is knowing when you can't be wise.
Muhammad Ali

I wanted to use my fame and this face that everyone knows so well to help uplift and inspire people around the world.
Muhammad Ali

When it comes to love compassion, and other feelings of the heart, I am rich.
Muhammad Ali

I am an ordinary man who worked hard to develop the talent I was given. I believed in myself and I believe in the goodness of others.
Muhammad Ali

We spend more time learning how to make a living than we do learning to make a life.
Muhammad Ali

I don't trust anyone who's nice to me but rude to the waiter. Because they would treat me the same way if I were in that position.
Muhammad Ali

My wealth is my knowledge of self, love, and spirituality.
Muhammad Ali

I've made my share of mistakes along the way, but if I have changed even one life for the better, I haven't lived in vain.
Muhammad Ali

When we devote all of our actions to a spiritual goal, everything that we do becomes a prayer.
Muhammad Ali

War of nations are fought to change maps. But wars of poverty are fought to map change.
Muhammad Ali

The greatest victory in life is to rise about the material things that we once valued most.
Muhammad Ali

Even the greatest was once a beginner. Don't be afraid to take that first step.
Muhammad Ali

Rest but never quit. Even the sun has a sinking spell each evening. But it always rises the next morning.
Muhammad Ali

I try to learn as much as I can because I know nothing compared to what I need to know.
Muhammad Ali

Old age is just a record of one's whole life.
Muhammad Ali

Everybody has talent, but ability takes hard work.
Michael Jordan

If I have an agenda or a goal, no one is going to deter me from what I want to do.
Michael Jordan

I've always believed that if you put in the work, the results will come.
Michael Jordan

Champions don't become champions when they win an event, but in the hours, weeks, months, and years they spend preparing for it.
Michael Jordan

Some people want it to happen, some wish it would happen, others make it happen.
Michael Jordan

Sometimes, things may not go your way, but the effort should be there every single night.
Michael Jordan

If you accept the expectations of others, especially negative ones, then you never will change the outcome.
Michael Jordan

One thing I believe to the fullest is that if you think and achieve as a team, the individual accolades will take care of themselves.
Michael Jordan

Obstacles don't have to stop you. If you run into a wall, don't turn around and give up. Figure out how to climb it, go through it, or work around it.
Michael Jordan

Unwillingness to sacrifice for the greater good of the team only makes individual goals more difficult to achieve.
Michael Jordan

Talent wins games, but teamwork and intelligence wins championships.
Michael Jordan

I can accept failure; everyone fails at something. But I can't accept not trying.
Michael Jordan

My attitude is that if you push me towards something that you think is a weakness, then I will turn that perceived weakness into a strength.
Michael Jordan

I've missed more than 9000 shots in my career. I've lost almost 300 games. 26 times, I've been trusted to take the game winning shot and missed. I've failed over and over and over again in my life. And that is why I succeed.
Michael Jordan

You must expect great things of yourself before you can do them.
Michael Jordan

To be successful you have to be selfish, or else you never achieve. And once you get to your highest level, then you have to be unselfish. Stay reachable. Stay in touch. Don't isolate.
Michael Jordan

To learn to succeed, you must first learn to fail.
Michael Jordan

Never say never, because limits, like fears, are often just an illusion.
Michael Jordan

Don't let them drag you down by rumors just go with what you believe in.
Michael Jordan

I'm not out there sweating for three hours every day just to find out what it feels like to sweat.
Michael Jordan

If you do the work you get rewarded. There are no shortcuts in life.
Michael Jordan

Once I made a decision, I never thought about it again.
Michael Jordan

The minute you get away from fundamentals — whether it's proper technique, work ethic or mental preparation — the bottom can fall out of your game, your schoolwork, your job, whatever you're doing.
Michael Jordan

If you quit once it becomes a habit. Never quit!
Michael Jordan

Always turn a negative situation into a positive situation.
Michael Jordan

The key to success is failure.
Michael Jordan

Learning's a gift, even when pain is your teacher.
Michael Jordan

Failure is acceptable. But not trying is a whole different ball park.
Michael Jordan

My body could stand the crutches but my mind couldn't stand the sideline.
Michael Jordan

I've never lost a game I just ran out of time.
Michael Jordan

Make it happen.
Michael Jordan

There is no "I" in team but there is in win.
Michael Jordan

The best comes from the worst.
Michael Jordan

I play to win, whether during practice or a real game.
Michael Jordan

I never looked at the consequences of missing a big shot. When you think about the consequences you will always think of the negative result.
Michael Jordan

The game is my wife. It demands loyalty and responsibility, and it gives me back fulfillment and peace.
Michael Jordan

I know fear is an obstacle for some people, but it is an illusion to me. Failure always made me try harder the next time.
Michael Jordan

It's heavy duty to try to do everything and please everybody. My job was to go out there and play the game of basketball as best I can. People may not agree with that. I can't live with what everyone's impression of what I should or what I shouldn't do
Michael Jordan

If it turns out that my best wasn't good enough, at least I won't look back and say I was afraid to try.
Michael Jordan

I realized that if I was going to achieve anything in life I had to be aggressive. I had to get out there and go for it.
Michael Jordan

Be true to the game, because the game will be true to you. If you try to shortcut the game, then the game will shortcut you. If you put forth the effort, good things will be bestowed upon you. That's truly about the game, and in some ways that's about life too.
Michael Jordan

Heart is what separates the good from the great.
Michael Jordan

I would tell players to relax and never think about what's at stake. Just think about the basketball game. If you start to think about who is going to win the championship, you've lost your focus.
Michael Jordan

You can practice shooting 8 hours a day, but if your technique is wrong, then all you become is very good at shooting the wrong way. Get the fundamentals down and the level of everything you do will rise.
Michael Jordan

I own the guy guarding me.
Michael Jordan

The game has its ups and downs, but you can never lose focus of your individual goals and you can't let yourself be beat because of lack of effort.
Michael Jordan

There is no such thing as a perfect basketball player, and I don't believe there is only one greatest player either.
Michael Jordan

I mean we all fly. Once you leave the ground, you fly. Some people fly longer than others.
Michael Jordan

Sometimes, things may not go your way, but the effort should be there every single night.
Michael Jordan

Best evaluation I can make of a player is to look in his eyes and see how scared they are.
Michael Jordan

Winning isn't always championships.
Michael Jordan

Sometimes you need to get hit in the head to realize that you're in a fight.
Michael Jordan

I want to wake up every day and do whatever comes in my mind, and not feel pressure or obligations to do anything else in my life.
Michael Jordan

Enjoy every minute of life. Never second-guess life.
Michael Jordan

I believe greatness is an evolutionary process that changes and evolves era to era.
Michael Jordan

If I had been playing for money, I would have complained a long time ago that I was underpaid.
Michael Jordan

Every time I feel tired while I am exercising and training, I close my eyes to see that picture, to see that list with my name. This usually motivates me to work again.
Michael Jordan

Being Michael Jordan means acting the same as I always have.
Michael Jordan

My heroes are and were my parents. I can't see having anyone else as my heroes.
Michael Jordan

In college I never realized the opportunities available to a pro athlete. I've been given the chance to meet all kinds of people, to travel and expand my financial capabilities, to get ideas and learn about life, to create a world apart from basketball.
Michael Jordan

My father used to say that it's never too late to do anything you wanted to do. And he said you never know what you can accomplish until you try.
Michael Jordan

When I will lose the sense of motivation and the sense to prove something as a basketball player, it's time for me to move away from the game.
Michael Jordan

I want to be the bridge to the next generation.
Michael Jordan

It's not about the shoes. It's about what you do in them.
Michael Jordan

I hope the millions of people I've touched have the optimism and desire to share their goals and hard work and perseverance with a positive attitude.
Michael Jordan

In reality, I never want to grow up.
Michael Jordan

How many times have your parents told you not to do things, and the next thing you know, you go do it? And you realized you shouldn't have done it.
Michael Jordan

For a competitive junkie like me, golf is a great solution because it smacks you in the face every time you think you've accomplished something. That to me has taken over a lot of the energy and competitiveness for basketball.
Michael Jordan

My challenge when I came back was to face the young talent, to dissect their games, and show them maybe that they needed to learn more about the game than just the money aspect.
Michael Jordan

Do I need my number retired throughout the course of the league to acknowledge what I've done? No.
Michael Jordan

I want to be perceived as a guy who played his best in all facets, not just scoring. A guy who love challenges.
Michael Jordan

I built my talents on the shoulders of someone else's talent.
Michael Jordan

Even when I'm old and gray, I won't be able to play it, but I'll still love the game.
Michael Jordan

I know the signs of scaredness.
Michael Jordan

You have competition every day because you set such high standards for yourself that you have to go out every day and live up to that.
Michael Jordan

It's absolutely wrong that I don't want guys to challenge me. And the people who say that aren't in the room.
Michael Jordan

Live the moment for the moment.
Michael Jordan

Just play. Have fun. Enjoy the game.
Michael Jordan

Earn your leadership every day.
Michael Jordan

CHAPTER 5

On Winning and Losing

Winning, like money, is an important motivation and scorecard. However, like money, winning isn't everything.

Likewise, while nobody likes or wants to lose, defeat is never an end-all event. People rebound and learn from all kinds of defeats and losses.

Opinions vary on the importance and value to be placed on winning. Is winning to be achieved "at all costs?" Do you believe "if you don't play to win, why keep the score?" Or is winning a matter of giving your best and making yourself better than yesterday?

What about losing? Is there value in losing? After all, losing can teach resiliency, sportsmanship, learning from mistakes, and valuing effort over results. All of which are important life skills.

Winning at all costs can have a tremendous negative impact. Witness the Volkswagen diesel emissions scandal. Rather than install a $350 component into each vehicle to meet the Clean Air Act regulations, engineers at this German auto manufacturer installed a software cheat device into over 11 million cars. This cheat device enabled Volkswagen, Audi, and Porsche vehicles to pass the EPA emissions test, at the same time that Volkswagen was misleading consumers with its Clean Diesel advertising campaign.

This "victory" has cost the Volkswagen Group over $35 billion to date in fines, penalties, and customer refunds. It has also led to the jailing of three of its executives in the U.S. and South Korea, with several others still under Department of Justice indictments.

Other companies whose employees and leaders have cheated their way to "winning" include Bosch, Mercedes-Benz, Deutsche Bank, Wells Fargo, HSBC, and many others.

Bending the rules, outright violations of laws and regulations, and plain old cheating are not the paths to winning. Instead, such actions turning winning into losing – big time!

Perhaps the best route for coaches and leaders is to encourage your team members to aim for winning and achieving desired results while accepting and appreciating the lessons that losing delivers.

My favorite quote from these words of wisdom on winning and losing is:

Winning takes talent; to repeat takes character.

John Wooden

Quotes On
Winning and Losing

Winning is not a sometime thing; it's an all-the-time thing. You don't win once in a while, you don't do things right once in a while, you do them right all the time. Winning is habit.
Vince Lombardi

The first time you quit, it's hard. The second time, it gets easier. The third time, you don't even have to think about it.
Paul (Bear) Bryant

Winning takes talent, to repeat takes character.
John Wooden

Before you can win, you have to believe you are worthy.
Mike Ditka

It's what you get from games you lose that is extremely important.
Pat Riley

Losers visualize the penalties of failure. Winners visualize the rewards of success.
Kobe Bryant

If winning isn't everything, why do they keep score?
Vince Lombardi

Setting a goal is not the main thing. It is deciding how you will go about achieving it and staying with that plan.
Tom Landry

Wisdom is always an overmatch for strength.
Phil Jackson

Never let your head hang down. Never give up and sit down and grieve. Find another way.
Satchel Paige

You have to believe in yourself when no one else does; that makes you a winner right there.
Venus Williams

Winners, I am convinced, imagine their dreams first. They want it with all their heart and expect it to come true.
Joe Montana

The trouble with being number one in the world – in anything – is that it takes a certain mentality to attain that once you do achieve number one, you don't relax and enjoy it.
Billie Jean King

It has nothing to do with talent, and everything to do with effort! Wins and losses come a dime a dozen. But effort? Nobody can judge that. Because effort is between you and you.
Ray Lewis

Achievement is largely the product of steadily raising one's levels of aspiration and expectation.
Jack Nicklaus

Part of being a champ is acting like a champ. You have to learn how to win and not run away when you lose. Everyone has bad stretches and real successes. Either way, you have to be careful not to lose your confidence or get too confident.
Nancy Kerrigan

I've never seen low-energy players be competitive.
Jeff Van Gundy

There's always the motivation of wanting to win — everybody has that — but a champion needs, in his attitude, a motivation above and beyond winning.
Pat Riley

If you believe in yourself, have dedication and pride and never quit, you'll be a winner.
Paul (Bear) Bryant

If I work on a certain move constantly, then finally, it doesn't seem risky to me. The idea is that the move stays dangerous and it looks dangerous to my foes, but it is not to me. Hard work has made it easy.
Nadia Comaneci

You learn you can do your best even when it's hard, even when you're tired and maybe hurting a little bit. It feels good to show some courage.
Joe Namath

Greats are totally emotionally independent.
Mike Tyson

How do you win? By getting average players to play good and good players to play great. That's how you win.
Oail Andrew [Bum] Phillips Jr.

The thrill isn't in the winning, it's in the doing.
Chuck Noll

You learn very little when you win.
Padraig Harrington

You have no choices about how you lose, but you do have a choice about how you come back and prepare to win again.
Pat Riley

Becoming number one is easier than remaining number one.
Bill Bradley

I've got a theory that if you give 100% all the time, somehow things will work out in the end.
Larry Bird

Being passive aggressive in this competition means you're fine with simply going with the flow and unwilling to disturb the calm waters of the game to accomplish your goals.
Kobe Bryant

If you don't practice you don't deserve to win.
Andre Agassi

One of the trademarks of a champion is that he can outlast you.
Lou Brock

Talent will get you to the top, but it takes character to keep you there.
John Wooden

The concentration and dedication — the intangibles — are the deciding factors between who won and who lost.
Tom Seaver

You have to perform at a consistently higher level than others. That's the mark of a true professional.
Joe Paterno

Show class, have pride and display character. If you do, winning takes care of itself.
Paul (Bear) Bryant

A champion is someone who gets up when he can't.
Jack Dempsey

One of life's most painful moments comes when we must admit that we didn't do our homework, that we are not prepared.
Merlin Olsen

You win some, you lose some, you wreck some.
Dale Earnhardt

What you lack in talent can be made up with desire, hustle and giving 110 percent all the time.
Don Zimmer

Only bad golfers are lucky. They're the ones bouncing balls off trees, curbs, turtles and cars. Good golfers have bad luck. When you hit the ball straight, a funny bounce is bound to be unlucky.
Lee Trevino

Champions keep playing until they get it right.
Billie Jean King

The man who wins, is the man who thinks he can.
Vince Lombardi

In every contest, there comes a moment that separates winning from losing. The true warrior understands and seizes that moment.
Pat Riley

There is no such thing as natural touch. Touch is something you create by hitting millions of golf balls.
Lee Trevino

Don't give up at halftime. Concentrate on winning the second half.
Paul (Bear) Bryant

Everyone has a plan 'till they get punched in the mouth.
Mike Tyson

There's nothing that cleanses your soul like getting the hell kicked out of you.
Woody Hayes

Win or lose, do it fairly.
Knute Rockne

Whatever the results you get, learn and grown from it and move on to the next one.
Dabo Swinney

If winning is God's reward, then losing is how he teaches us.
Serena Williams

No one has as much luck around the greens as one who practices a lot.
Chi Chi Rodriguez

Always make a total effort, even when the odds are against you.
Arnold Palmer

Winners embrace hard work. They love the discipline of it, the trade-off they're making to win. Losers, on the other hand, see it as punishment. And that's the difference.
Lou Holtz

Concentration and mental toughness are the margins of victory.
Bill Russell

To be a champ you have to believe in yourself when no one else will.
Sugar Ray Robinson

When you miss a shot, never think of what you did wrong. Take the next shot thinking of what you must do right.
Tony Alfonso

Did I win? Did I lose? Those are the wrong questions. The correct question is: Did I make my best effort? That's what matters. The rest of it just gets in the way.
John Wooden

I am building a fire, and every day I train, I add more fuel. At just the right moment, I light the match.
Mia Hamm

You put out, you suck up your gut, give it all you've got and you give me that second effort. You give me that much and I'll show you glory.
Paul (Bear) Bryant

You're carrying a legacy. You're carrying greatness. And greatness is a lot of small things done well. Day after day. Workout after workout. Obedience after obedience.
Ray Lewis

To uncover your true potential, you must first find your own limits, and then you have to have the courage to blow past them.
Picabo Street

The key to a winning season is focusing on one opponent at a time. Winning one week at a time. Never look back and never look ahead.
Chuck Noll

There's always a point where you get knocked down. But I draw on what I've learned on the track: If you work hard, things will work out.
Lolo Jones

I don't run away from a challenge because I am afraid. Instead, I run toward it because the only way to escape fear is to trample it beneath your feet.
Nadia Comaneci

The man who complains about the way the ball bounces is likely to be the one who dropped it.
Lou Holtz

The moment you give up, is the moment you let someone else win.
Kobe Bryant

Know how to win by following the rules.
Arnold Palmer

I don't like to lose — at anything — yet I've grown most not from victories, but setbacks.
Serena Williams

Hustle beats muscle when muscle doesn't hustle.
Jon Gordon

I'm a dreamer. I have to dream and reach for the stars, and if I miss a star then I grab a handful of clouds.
Mike Tyson

Part of being a champ is acting like a champ. You have to learn how to win and not run away when you lose.
Nancy Kerrigan

The real glory is being knocked to your knees and the coming back. That's real glory. That's the essence of it.
Vince Lombardi

What does it take to be a champion? Desire, dedication, determination, concentration and the will to win.
Patty Berg

There are only two options regarding commitment. You're either IN or you're OUT. There's no such thing as life in between.
Pat Riley

What makes something special is not just what you have to gain, but what you feel there is to lose.
Andre Agassi

Players that have ENERGY when they're on the bench are far more likely to impact games in a positive way when they're in the game.
Tom Crean

There are no office hours for champions.
Paul Dietzel

Most important ingredient to winning: no personal agendas. The commitment has to be "us" driven not "me" driven.
Kevin Eastman

Respect every opponent, but fear none.
John Wooden

Life's battles don't always go to the stronger or faster man. Sooner or later the man who wins is the man who thinks he can.
Vince Lombardi

I'd rather have preparation than motivation. Everyone likes to play, but no one likes to practice.
Bum Phillips

Champions are champions not because they do anything extraordinary but because they do ordinary things better than anyone else.
Chuck Noll

It's not about what you say. It's about how you play the game. Most of the time it's just doing what you do at a higher level.
Brad Stevens

Adversity is not the opportunity to make excuses.
Dabo Swinney

It is not a dreamlike state, but the somehow insulated state, that a great musician achieves in a great performance. He's aware of where he is and what he's doing, but his mind is on the playing of the instrument with an internal sense of rightness.
Arnold Palmer

Competing at the highest level is not about winning. It's about preparation, courage, understanding, and nurturing your people, and heart. Winning is the result.
Joe Torre

If you are going to play soft, you are playing into the other team's hands. Be nice off the court. On the court, get a little nasty.
Jeff Hornacek

You can make all the excuses you want, but if you're not mentally tough and you're not prepared to play every night, you're not going to win.
Larry Bird

I learned this a long time ago: your two best players have got to be winning players. Winning is their number one objective.
Hubie Brown

It will come down to who will be the toughest the longest.
Mack Brown

Every day we need to be one step up from where we were the day before.
Geno Auriemma

Champions never complain, they are too busy getting better.
John Wooden

You really shouldn't have to beg a basketball player for energy, effort, or unselfishness. That's just how you win.
Jeff Van Gundy

Don't succumb to excuses. Go back to the job of making the corrections and forming the habits that will make your goal possible.
Vince Lombardi

There's one thing about quitters you have to guard against —they are contagious.
Paul (Bear) Bryant

At one point in your life, you either have the thing you want or the reasons why you don't.
Andy Roddick

Everyone is born with a certain potential. You may never achieve your full potential, but how close you come depends on how much you want to pay the price.
Red Auerbach

Winning isn't everything, but it beats anything that comes in second.
Paul (Bear) Bryant

We do not win championships with girls. We win with competitors.
Pat Summitt

Don't let a single game break your heart.
Mike Krzyzewski

We compete not so much against an opponent, but against ourselves. The real test is: did I make my best effort on every play?
Bud Wilkinson

Handling adversity is just as much about attitude as it is action. Those who can stay clam in adverse situations can usually overcome them.
Derek Jones

You must believe that you are the best. And then, make sure that you are.
Bill Shankly

You never win a game unless you beat the guy in front of you. The score on the board doesn't mean a thing. That's for the fans. You've got to win the war with the man in front of you. You've got to get your man.
Vince Lombardi

Players that make excuses in the summer for why they can't work out are usually hard at work in season blaming others for failure.
Tom Crean

Every game you step on the court, you should think it's a big game.
Jeff Hornacek

Almost always, your road to victory goes through a place called failure.
Bill Walsh

A winner is somebody who goes out there every day and exhausts himself trying to get something accomplished.
Joe Torre

The only way to prove that you're a good sport is to lose.
Ernie Banks

I think a champion is defined not by their wins but by how they can recover when they fall.
Serena Williams

Winning takes precedence over all. There's no gray area. No almost.
Kobe Bryant

The time your game is most vulnerable is when you're ahead. Never let up.
Rod Laver, Adidas

Tactics, fitness, stroke ability, adaptability, experience, and sportsmanship are all necessary for winning.
Fred Perry

Second place is meaningless. You can't always be first, but you have to believe that you should have been.
Vince Lombardi

First become a winner in life. Then it's easier to become a winner on the field.
Tom Landry

When the legs go, the heart soon follows.
John Wooden

Some nights, you got to lose with your star player. You don't always win with him. You got to lose with him.
Chuck Daly

Winning is not complicated. People complicate it. Consistent winning motivation comes from within.
Dick Vermeil

First, there are those who are winners and know they are winners. Then there are the losers who know they are losers. Then there are those who are not winners, but don't know it. They're the ones for me. They never quit trying. They're the soul of our game.
Paul (Bear) Bryant

Win or lose you will never regret working hard, making sacrifices, being disciplined, or focusing too much. Success is measured by what we have done to prepare for competition.
John Walton Smith

I don't care about the result. I just care that we have no regrets. The pain of discipline isn't as bad as the pain of regret.
Brad Stevens

BIG-TIME players make BIG-TIME plays in BIG-TIME games.
Jimmy Johnson

We win our games in practice. We learn and follow the fundamentals of our game better than anyone in the league. All of our games are won in practice.
Vince Lombardi

Never get rattled. Answer a big play with a big play.
Bill Self

In my experience, you learn far more from winning, which also makes your players more receptive to criticism.
Bill Parcells

The only thing even is the number of hours in a day. The difference in winning or losing is what you do with those hours.
Woody Hayes

You must play boldly to win.
Arnold Palmer

If you think you are good, think you are the best, you better go out there and beat the best.
Mike Ditka

Remember that basketball is a game of habits. If you make the other guy deviate from his habits, you've got him.
Bill Russell

To defeat a weak opponent is not the problem. The problem is to win when he is as good or better than you.
Robert Neyland

Winning isn't everything, but wanting to win is.
Vince Lombardi

The best attitudes in the world won't help win ball games if they're not accompanied by a fundamental competence in the game.
Dr. Jack Ramsay

Losing is only temporary and not encompassing. You must simply study it, learn from it, and try hard not to lose the same way again. Then you must have the self-control to forget about it.
John Wooden

You can't win every game, but you can learn from every game.
Mike Krzyzewski

The first thing you have to do to win is make sure you don't beat yourself.
Chuck Noll

It's awfully important to win with humility. It's also important to lose. I hate to lose worse than anyone, but if you never lose you won't know how to act. If you lose with humility, then you can come back.
Paul (Bear) Bryant

About the only problem with success is that it does not teach you how to deal with failure.
Tommy Lasorda

You have people telling you how good you are and all of a sudden, you start believing it and forget what it takes to be good.
Lou Lamoriello

Most players want to be winners, but it is the degree of commitment that determines the extent they will exceed.
Jack Gardner

In order to be a winner, you have to look for ways of getting things done and not for reasons why things can't be done. People who live with excuses have things that can't be done hovering around them all the time.
Mike Krzyzewski

Winners embrace hard work. They love the discipline of it, the trade-off they're making to win. Losers see it as punishment.
Lou Holtz

A champion pays an extra price to be better than anyone else.
Paul (Bear) Bryant

A man can be as great as he wants to be. If you believe in yourself and have the courage, the determination, the dedication, the competitive drive and if you are willing to sacrifice the little things in life and pay the price for the things that are worthwhile, it can be done.
Vince Lombardi

There is only a half-step difference between the champions and those who finish on the bottom. And much of that half step is mental.
Tom Landry

No one plays this or any game perfectly. It's the guy who recovers from his mistakes who wins.
Phil Jackson

There are no magic plays. You win based on effort, unmet focus and being brilliant at the little details.
Steve Kerr

You must win this minute. You must win this day. And tomorrow will take care of itself.
John Chaney

Champions are champions not because they do anything extraordinary but because they do ordinary things better than anyone else.
Chuck Noll

Remember, your attitude toward a situation can help you to change it—you create the very atmosphere for defeat or victory.
Franco Harris

Giving all, it seems to me, is not so far from victory.
George Moriarty

Champions do not become champions on the court. They become recognized on the court. They become champions because of their daily routine and commitment to excellence. Players do not decide their future; they decide their habits and their habits decide their future!
Kevin Eastman

The scoreboard will take care of itself. Winning and losing is getting these guys to reach their full potential. It's giving them the tools to go out in life and be really successful.
Matt Campbell

You are never a loser until you quit trying.
Mike Ditka

Becoming a champion is not an easy process. It is done by focusing on what it takes to get there and not on getting there.
Nick Saban

You carry on no matter what are the obstacles. You simply refuse to give up - and, when the going gets tough, you get tougher. And, you win.
Vince Lombardi

Friends hang from time to time. Banners hang forever.
Kobe Bryant

To finish first, you must first finish.
Rick Mears

Victory is very, very sweet. It tastes better than and desert you've ever had.
Serena Williams

The spirit, the will to win, and the will to excel are the things that endure. These qualities are so much more important than the events that occur.
Vince Lombardi

CHAPTER 6

Success

Thanks to the self-help and personal development industries, there are probably more words written on success than any other subject. And, as you might imagine, there are as many definitions of success as there are authors.

The best definition of success, in my opinion, comes from legendary UCLA basketball coach John Wooden:

> *"Success is peace of mind which is a direct*
> *result of self-satisfaction in knowing you did*
> *your best to become the best that you are*
> *capable of becoming."*

I see success as the on-going process of becoming better...of striving to become the best that you are truly capable of being in whatever endeavors you choose. Successful people are always expanding and improving themselves – intellectually, spiritually, emotionally, and physically.

Success requires a personal commitment to excellence. Here are some of the tips I give to my coaching clients on taking the right steps toward success:

- Add value to everything you do — every time.

- Combine inspiration with perspiration, even

if this is only "mental perspiration."

- Understand that one of the greatest differences between success and failure is that successful people tackle the chores and dirty work that others do not.

- Excellence never comes from work done hastily, short cuts, or careless attention to details. And it is rarely produced by last-minutes or under the pressure of deadlines.

- Every small task or detail, no matter how minute or seemingly insignificant, is important if it is part of your work or has the potential to impact your output. The difference between mediocrity and excellence is often in the attention to detail.

- Live in "prime time" rather than watching prime time TV.

- Aim not for what you are. Aim not for what you can be without effort. Aim for what you could be and desire to be.

- The achievement of one goal is simply the starting point for another. Build upon each achievement to climb your own personal ladder of success.

Successful people are opportunity minded. Do not be problem minded. Problems are merely opportunities clothed to deceive. Nourish your opportunities and give sufficient attention to problems to turn them into recognizable and attainable opportunities.

Each of us has options about what we will do with our lives and what we will make of ourselves. However, no matter what paths we choose and what options we select, once those decisions are made, we have two choices:

1) To be less than what we have the capacity to become, or

2) To be all that we can be, to strive as best we can with the skills we have and the circumstances given.

Successful people also have a great responsibility to pay back to society for the fruits they enjoy. This is done by contributing to their communities, to a global cause such as the environment or starvation, or by sharing their knowledge and skills through coaching and mentoring. How will you give back to society based on your success in life?

My favorite quotation from these words of wisdom on success is:

Celebrate what you have accomplished
but raise the bar a little higher
each time you succeed.

Mia Hamm

Quotes on Success

I've observed that if individuals who prevail in highly competitive environments have any one thing in common besides success, it is failure — and their ability to overcome it.
Bill Walsh

If what you did yesterday still looks big today, you haven't done much today.
Mike Krzyzewski

The highest compliment that you can pay me is to say that I work hard every day, that I never dog it.
Wayne Gretzky

To be successful, you must dedicate yourself 100% to your training, diet and mental approach.
Arnold Schwarzenegger

I didn't have the same fitness or ability as the other girls, so I had to beat them with my mind.
Martina Hingis

Sooner or later, you have to stand up and get something done. They're always hearing about what their predecessors did, but I told them [before the game], this is your chance to do something your predecessors haven't done.
Tom Izzo

Success is anything worthwhile. It has a price. You have to pay the price to win and you have to pay the price to get to the point where success is possible. Most important, you must pay the price to stay there.
Vince Lombardi

Success isn't measured by money or power or social rank. Success is measured by your discipline and inner peace.
Mike Ditka

Confidence is the most important single factor in this game, and no matter how great your natural talent, there is only one way to obtain and sustain it: work.
Jack Nicklaus

Success is that peace of mind that comes from knowing you've done everything in your power to become the very best you're capable of becoming.
John Wooden

It isn't hard to be good from time to time. What is tough is being good every day.
Willie Mays

We can always kind of be average and do what's normal. I'm not in this to do what's normal.
Kobe Bryant

If everything seems under control, you're just not going fast enough.
Mario Andretti

Once you agree upon the price you and your family must pay for success, it enables you to ignore the minor hurts, the opponent's pressure, and the temporary failures.
Vince Lombardi

I'm playing the guys who are going to fight. If you're not into this, I'm going to someone else.
John Calipari

Success at the highest level comes down to one question: Can you decide that your happiness can come from someone else's success?
Bill Walton

The most important key to achieving great success is to decide upon your goal and launch, get started, take action, move.
John Wooden

The best part about passion and why it is so important to success is that passion allows us to put ourselves out there even when we know that failure may be the result.
Kevin Eastman

The overnight sensation understands better than anyone else that success never comes overnight.
Ian Thomsen

To be successful, you have to learn to do things you don't like. You find ways to like the process and make the most of that time.
Mike Krzyzewski

There may be people that have more talent than you, but there's no excuse for anyone to work harder than you do.
Derek Jeter

If you are afraid of failure you don't deserve to be successful!
Charles Barkley

I don't think that once you get to one level, you can relax. You've got to keep pushing.
Larry Bird

When you come to practice, you cease to exist as an individual. You're part of a team.
John Wooden

If you want to be good, you really don't have a lot of choices, because it takes what it takes.
Nick Saban

The difference between a successful person and others is not a lack of strength, not a lack of knowledge, but rather a lack in will.
Vince Lombardi

The will to succeed is important, but what's more important is the will to prepare.
Bobby Knight

My confidence comes from the daily grind — training my butt off day in and day out.
Hope Solo

When we are saying this cannot be accomplished, this cannot be done, then we are short-changing ourselves. My brain, it cannot process failure. It will not process failure. Because if I have to sit there and face myself and tell myself 'you are a failure,' I think that is almost worse than dying.
Kobe Bryant

You miss 100% of the shots you never take.
Wayne Gretzky

The key to success is to learn to do something right and then do it right every time.
Pat Riley

People of mediocre ability sometimes achieve outstanding success because they don't know when to quit.
George Allen Sr.

Set your goals high and don't stop till you get there.
Bo Jackson

My hunger is not for success, it is for excellence. Because when you attain excellence, success just naturally follows.
Mike Krzyzewski

Celebrate what you've accomplished but raise the bar a little higher each time you succeed.
Mia Hamm

Never be a spectator while in the game. Be doing something at all times, even if it is only a decoy.
John Wooden

I believe your attitude is the most important choice you can make.
Lou Holtz

Do you want to be safe and good, or do you want to take a chance and be great?
Jimmy Johnson

Stay focused. Your start does not determine how you're going to finish.
Herm Edwards

There are three types of baseball players: those who make it happen, those who watch it happen, and those who wonder what happens.
Tommy Lasorda

If you don't want to be coached, then you don't want to be great!
Ryan Pannone

Run towards expectation, run towards pressure and you have a better chance at success.
Joe Maddon

Be great at the things that take no talent.
Brad Stevens

I start early and I stay late, day after day, year after year, it took me 17 years and 114 days to become an overnight success.
Lionel Messi

In order to excel, you must be completely dedicated to your chosen sport. You must also be prepared to work hard and be willing to accept constructive criticism.
Willie Mays

If you have a positive attitude and constantly strive to give your best effort, eventually you will overcome your immediate problems and find you are ready for greater challenges.
Pat Riley

If Plan A isn't working, I have Plan B, Plan C, and even Plan D.
Serena Williams

The key to success is to keep growing in all areas of life – mental, emotional, spiritual, as well as physical.
Julius Erving

When you are passionate, you always have your destination in sight and you are not distracted by obstacles. Because you love what you are pursuing, things like rejection and setbacks will not hinder you in your pursuit. You believe that nothing can stop you!
Mike Krzyzewski

There is only one way to succeed in anything and that is to give it everything.
Vince Lombardi

Limits are self-imposed. But there are no limits to human energy nor the goals you can achieve.
Mike Shanahan

Success comes from knowing that you did your best to become the best that you are capable of becoming.
John Wooden

Luck has nothing to do with it, I have spent many, many hours, countless hours, on the court working for my one moment in time, not knowing when it would come.
Serena Williams

Your body language is a billboard for your mental toughness and maturity.
Ron Naclerio

Coach showed he believed in me. So I had to believe in myself.
Rajon Rondo

Playing without the fundamentals is like eating without a knife and fork. You make a mess.
Dick Williams

Tomorrow is yet to come. However, tomorrow is, in large part, determined by what you do today.
John Wooden

When you make a choice and say "come hell or high water" I am going to be this, then you should not be surprised when you are that. It should not be something that feels intoxicating or out of character because you have seen this moment for so long that...when that moment comes, of course it is here because it has been here the whole time because it has been in your mind the whole time.
Kobe Bryant

When opportunity comes, it's too late to prepare.
John Wooden

At the end of the day, you have to go out on the grass and perform.
Kirby Smart

The thing that can separate you is the love of competition, not the love of the lifestyle. Putting yourself out there where you're not running for most-liked player, but most-respected, because of how hard you're willing to compete.
Jeff Van Gundy

It's hard to work really hard at something if you don't live it. I don't care what line of work you're in.
Scott Frost

If you didn't get it done yesterday get it done today.
Tim S. Grover

Experience shows that success is due less to ability than to zeal. The winner is he who gives himself to his work, body and soul.
Tony Dorsett

If you're five minutes early, you're already ten minutes late.
Vince Lombardi

Attitude is a choice. What you think you can do, whether positive or negative, confident or scared, will most likely happen.
Pat Summitt

A successful person never loses — they either win or learn.
John Calipari

Two kinds of ballplayers aren't worth a darn: one that never does what he's told and one who does nothing except what he's told.
Bum Philips

The beauty in being blessed with talent is rising above doubters to create a beautiful moment.
Kobe Bryant

Never be the player whose body language is louder than your voice.
Tom Crean

Competitiveness is not emotion and anger after the fact; it is the amount of effort in preparation.
Mano Watsa

You've got to earn it. You can't count on other people to do your job for you.
Herm Edwards

If you believe in yourself and have dedication and pride — and never quit — you'll be a winner. The price of victory is high but so are the rewards.
Paul (Bear) Bryant

Everybody wants to do it. Not everybody is willing to do what they have to do to do it.
Nick Saban

Pain doesn't tell you when you ought to stop. Pain is the little voice in your head that tries to hold you back because it knows if you continue you will change. Don't let it stop you from being who you can be. Exhaustion tells you when you ought to stop. You only reach your limit when you can go no further.
Kobe Bryant

In any game, you do the things you do best and you do them over and over and over.
George Halas

The price of success is hard work, dedication to the job at hand, and the determination that whether we win or lose, we have applied the best of ourselves to the task at hand.
Vince Lombardi

The two hardest things to handle in life are failure and success.
John Wooden

Run from being good. Chase being great.
Chip Kelly

The preparation process makes the experience fulfilling. No preparation means no foundation to build on in the future.
John Stockton

Ambition is the path to success. Persistence is the vehicle you arrive in.
Bill Bradley

I think the thing about that was I was always willing to work; I was not the fastest or biggest player but I was determined to be the best football player I could be on the football field and I think I was able to accomplish that through hard work.
Jerry Rice

It's simple really: be great right now so that you can be great later on.
Peter Carroll

In a highly competitive environment, feeling comfortable is first cousin to being complacent.
Bill Walsh

Accept false steps as opportunities to learn. It's one thing to hate failure, it's another to fear it.
Bill Parcells

Bad players want to show the world what they can't do. Good players stay within themselves and do what they can do.
Bob Huggins

You can only achieve that which you will do.
George Halas

Mistakes come from doing, but so does success.
John Wooden

The harder you work, the harder it is to surrender.
Vince Lombardi

Success is where preparation and opportunity meet.
Bobby Unser

Being a professional is doing the things you love to do, on the days you don't feel like doing them.
Julius Erving

You're entitled to absolutely nothing is this game. If you want it. You've got to work for it.
Doc Rivers

If you are always striving to achieve success defined by someone else; you'll always be frustrated. Define your own success.
Mike Krzyzewski

That's what this game is. It's a grind. You got to love the grind. You got to stay in the grind.
John Calipari

I have self-doubt. I have insecurity. I have fear of failure. I have nights when I show up at the arena and I'm like, "My back hurts, my feet hurt, my knees hurt. I don't have it. I just want to chill." We all have self-doubt. You don't deny it, but you also don't capitulate to it. You embrace it.
Kobe Bryant

I think you've got to pay the price for anything that's worthwhile, and success is paying the price. You've got to pay the price to win, you've got to pay the price to stay on top, and you've got to pay the price to get there.
Vince Lombardi

Never believe talent is only ABILITY you need. You need SUSTAINABILITY, DURABILITY, RELIABILITY and COACHABILITY to have true success.
Tom Crean

The goal here has always been to focus on the things we can control. Which are: how we play, how we perform and how we prepare.
Nick Saban

Success isn't all about talent. It's about being dependable, consistent, coachable, and knowing what you need to do to improve.
Bill Belichick

You can do one of two things: You can humble yourself or life will humble you. I think it's a lot easier to find a way to humble yourself.
Billy Donovan

Sustaining a level of execution from the beginning of practice to the end. That is the best way to learn to play a complete game.
David Cutcliffe

The main thing I'd say is attitude. You can always do something to help your attitude.
Scotty Bowman

You should never be proud of doing the right thing. You should just do it.
Dean Smith

Are you going to focus on what you did, or on what you are going to do?
Nick Saban

Often when things are at their worst you're closer than you can imagine to success.
Bill Walsh

Once you learn to quit, it becomes a habit.
Vince Lombardi

Every player should take five minutes to themselves before practice and mentally lock into what needs to be done.
Jeff Boals

We compete not so much against an opponent, but against ourselves. The real test is: Did I make my best effort on every play?
Bud Wilkinson

Integrity doesn't come in degrees: low, medium, or high. You either have integrity or you don't.
Tony Dungy

It's my experience that people rise to the level of their own expectations and of the competition they seek out.
Pat Summitt

I can't relate to lazy people. We don't speak the same language. I don't understand you. I don't want to understand you.
Kobe Bryant

Roles don't come from a job description. There's more to them than physical skill. They evolve within the context of the team.
Bill Bradley

The only thing you deserve is what you earn.
Tom Brands

The man who is afraid to risk failure seldom has to face success.
John Wooden

I don't care what you did yesterday. If you're happy with that, you have bigger problems.
Nick Saban

The competitor who won't go away, who won't stay down, has one of the most formidable competitive advantages of all.
Bill Walsh

Are you playing to win or are you playing 'Not to lose?'
John Calipari

I think my whole career, the thing that drove me to try to do things right, was the fear that I would fail, not only myself, but fail a player.
Sparky Anderson

If it's important to you, you will find a way. If it's not you will find an excuse.
Davey Whitney

You don't have any chance to succeed until you learn how to compete.
Seth Greenberg

Basketball is a we game; not a me game. Do you play for the scoreboard or the scorebook?
Kevin Eastman

A player who makes a team great is more valuable than a great player.
John Wooden

Taking ownership. Players have to do that. The best programs are player-run.
James Franklin

I won't accept anything less than the best a player's capable of doing, and he has the right to expect the best I can do for him.
Lou Holtz

Complacency is the forerunner of mediocrity. You can never work too hard on attitudes, effort and technique.
Don Meyer

If you're gonna be great, you can't ever be satisfied.
Dabo Swinney

Commitment separates those who live their dreams from those who live life regretting the opportunities they've squandered.
Bill Russell

It's about being relentless in the pursuit of your goal and resilient in the face of bad luck and adversity.
Nick Saban

Self-praise is for losers. Be a winner. Stand for something. Always have class, and be humble.
John Madden

Don't do anything as an individual that will make you stand out from your teammates.
Mike Krzyzewski

For when the One Great Scorer comes to mark against your name, He writes — not that you won or lost — but how you played the Game.
Grantland Rice

Consider the rights of others before your own feelings, and the feelings of others before your own rights.
John Wooden

For me the starting point for everything - before strategy, tactics, theories, managing, organizing, philosophy, methodology, talent, or experience - is work ethic.
Bill Walsh

Play and practice like you are trying to make the team.
Mike Krzyzewski

Most opportunities don't immediately bring results. Often times, they only lead to more opportunities.
Buzz Williams

When your best player puts it on the line every day, the other guys can't cut corners.
George Karl

Spectacular achievements come from unspectacular preparation.
Roger Staubach

With the absence of pressure, it's hard to do great things.
Geno Auriemma

If you're aware and you're high-energy, the ball will eventually bounce your way and you'll be able to make plays.
Jeremy Lin

I always say you should be very careful with the voices you listen to. And my closest voices have always told me, "You can."
Becky Hammon

If you work harder than somebody else, chances are you'll beat him though he has more talent than you.
Bart Starr

If I fail, I'm coming back. If I fail again, I'm coming back stronger.
Devean George

Discipline helps you finish a job, and finishing is what separates excellent work from average work.
Pat Summitt

My motto was always to keep swinging. Whether I was in a slump or feeling badly or having trouble off the field, the only thing to do was keep swinging.
Hank Aaron

Don't let others decide who you are.
Dennis Rodman

Success isn't determined by how many times you win, but by how you play the week after you lose.
Pelé

Today, you have 100% of your life left.
Tom Landry

Earn the right to be proud and confident.
John Wooden

Nobody who ever gave his best regretted it.
George Halas

Enjoying success requires the ability to adapt. Only by being open to change will you have a true opportunity to get the most from your talent.
Nolan Ryan

Who wins the battle when you're tired?
Shaka Smart

Instead of moping and complaining — go to work.
Tom Izzo

Personal Development

Your personal development as a coach is your own responsibility – not that of the organization you work for, your boss, the HR department, or anyone else.

It is time to stop waiting for your company to develop your leadership and coaching skills. Likewise, stop wasting time on university programs full of theory but no practicality. Be proactive. Start leading and controlling your own personal and professional development.

Additionally, you should never wait for anyone to tell you how to develop yourself. Besides, you probably have a pretty good inkling as to your development areas. As Master Jedi Yoda stated in one of the *Star Wars* films, *"Already know you that which you need."*

When it comes to personal and professional development, most people focus on their gap areas. I encourage you to understand your strengths and use them to leverage your performance and overshadow your coaching skill gaps.

Managing and motivating yourself as an individual contributor differs greatly from managing and motivating other team members. This is why the leadership training programs for senior leaders cannot easily cascade down to new supervisors and mid-level leaders. You need programs specifically tailored to your responsibilities, challenges, difficulties, and concerns.

As a leader, you can only be effective as a coach when given optimal development and training opportunities that enable you to lead for results, lead diverse groups of people, lead the development of people, and lead your own development and growth.

To develop your leadership skills, seek leadership education, not a training program. Almost all leadership training programs have one inherent flaw – you do not get to speak or interact with your trainer after the program concludes. So, you have no one to answer your questions. No one to bounce ideas off. And no one to help you assess how well you are implementing and applying the skills and tools you were taught.

Well, I have fixed that. A key component of our 8-part online leadership education program, called *The Art of Great Leadership*, includes 24 months of small-group coaching sessions. These 60-90-minute coaching sessions are all recorded if you cannot attend a session or if you ever want to back and review a discussion. See the Resources section at the back of this book for the link to *The Art of Great Leadership* website.

Here are some proven best-practice tips for working on your personal or professional development:

- Work on only one or two at a time so you don't bite off more than you can chew!
- Take baby steps and build momentum as you

progress

- Practice, practice, practice
- Leverage your strengths
- Treat setback as evidence that you have not (yet) developed expertise in a particular skill area – not as a sign that you are not cut out to be a coach
- Focus on improvement over perfection
- Focus on process over results – recognize your efforts and reward your results
- Focus on the positives over the negatives
- Keep an open mind – personal development is a journey

One last thought, which is one of my own quotes: Never stop learning, for life never stops teaching.

Here is my favorite quote from the words of wisdom in this section on personal development:

Admit to and make yourself accountable for mistakes. How can you improve if you're never wrong?

Pat Summitt

Quotes on Personal Development

I know what I have to do, and I'm going to do whatever it takes. If I do it, I'll come out a winner, and it doesn't matter what anyone else does.
Florence Griffith Joyner

You are never really playing an opponent. You are playing yourself, and when you reach your limits, that is real joy.
Arthur Ashe

If you learn to use it right, the adversity, it will buy you a ticket to a place you couldn't have gone any other way.
Tony Bennett

There is always space for improvement, no matter how long you've been in the business.
Oscar De La Hoya

Whatever you do in life, surround yourself with smart people who'll argue with you.
John Wooden

What to do with a mistake:
• Recognize It
• Admit It
• Learn From It
• Forget It
Dean Smith

Excellence is not an accomplishment. It is a spirit, a never-ending process.
Lawrence M. Miller

In order to be a winner, you have to look for ways of getting things done and not for reasons why things can't be done.
Mike Krzyzewski

I'm reflective only in the sense that I learn to move forward. I reflect with a purpose.
Kobe Bryant

Discipline is not a dirty word.
Pat Riley

Good talent with bad attitude equals bad talent.
Bill Walsh

Admit to and make yourself accountable for mistakes. How can you improve if you're never wrong?
Pat Summitt

Don't succumb to excuses. Go back to the job of making the corrections and forming the habits that will make your goal possible.
Vince Lombardi

Hustle makes up for many a mistake.
John Wooden

You never stay the same. You either get better or you get worse.
Jon Gruden

Never be comfortable with just good enough.
Ray Lewis

If you train badly, you play badly. If you work like a beast in training, you play the same way.
Pep Guardiola

If you don't have a plan for success then you do have a plan to fail.
Steve Keating

Define your unique talent or gift, develop it to the fullest, and give it away every day.
Don Meyer

Being coachable is on the player. If you want to win you will be coachable.
Jeff Van Gundy

Being the best you can be is something that you can personally evaluate. After all, who better can determine if you truly did your best? And, having pride means never settling for less.
Nick Saban

There is no substitute for hard work. If you're looking for the easy way, if you're looking for the trick, you might get by for a while, but you will not be developing the talents that lie within you. There is simply no substitute for work.
John Wooden

Train the way you're gonna play.
Dwayne Ledford

Before anything great is really achieved, your comfort zone must be disturbed.
Ray Lewis

If you go as far as you can see, you will then see enough to go even farther.
John Wooden

If you strive for perfection, it doesn't matter who the opponent is. You're playing against yourself.
Vince Kehres

Anything worthy of your passion, should be worthy of your preparation.
Sue Enquist

Excellence happens when you try, each day, to both do and be a little better than you were yesterday.
Pat Riley

Don't be afraid to fail. Experience is just mistakes you don't make anymore.
Joe Garagiola

If you think you are one of your team's top leaders or players you have to be receptive to being pushed and coached harder than others.
Tom Crean

Don't measure yourself by what you have accomplished, but by what you should have accomplished with your ability.
John Wooden

Mental toughness is spartanism with qualities of sacrifice, self-denial, dedication. It is fearlessness, and it is love.
Vince Lombardi

Good things take time, as they should. We shouldn't expect good things to happen overnight. Actually, getting something too easily or too soon can cheapen the outcome.
John Wooden

Adversity is not the opportunity to make excuses.
Dabo Swinney

Be the best version of yourself. Have passion, a great attitude, a single-minded focus, relentless energy, and always finish.
Jason Garrett

Discipline to me is sacrifice; it's willingness to give up something you want to do, so you can better yourself.
Bobby Bowden

There are always those times when you're going to be down, it's how you step through it that makes you the person you are.
Mike Krzyzewski

No one's ever gotten better by practicing less.
Ron Jaworski

Mistakes are the necessary steps in the learning process; once they have served their purpose, they should be forgotten and not repeated.
Vince Lombardi

Sometimes all you need is just for somebody to believe in you in order to be able to accomplish maybe what you never thought you could.
Drew Brees

You can make mistakes, but you're not a failure until you start blaming others for those mistakes.
John Wooden

Nothing is work unless you'd rather be doing something else.
George Halas

Always told my players there are 5 things EVERY player can control that has ZERO to do with talent:
1. Be on time
2. Play with GREAT effort
3. Maintain good body language
4. Bring Positive Energy/Attitude
5. Be Coachable.
Gene Chizik

I think sometimes the best training is to rest.
Cristiano Ronaldo

Don't look for the big, quick improvement. Seek the small improvement one day at a time. That's the only way it happens, and when it happens, it lasts.
John Wooden

Either you use an experience to help build you and make you better, or the experience breaks you.
John Calipari

You maximize your potential by being humble, developing a work ethic, striving to be a good person, and to be the best teammate you can be.
Steve Nash

You get better when your best effort becomes your way of life.
Tom Crean

If coaches are pushing you hard, be thankful for it means they care. Be worried if and when they stop.
Steven Howard

To go from good to great, it's all in the details. Everything matters.
Steve Kerr

You only gain confidence through experience, and the harder the experience that you're successful in, the more confidence you get.
Mike Krzyzewski

I figure practice puts your brains in your muscles.
Sam Snead

Freshmen come in thinking, 'if I can score, I can play.' They quickly find out if they can defend, they'll play.
Steve Fisher

It's normal to enjoy praise and dislike criticism. True character is when you prevent either from affecting you in a negative manner.
John Wooden

Practice does not make perfect; perfect practice makes perfect.
Vince Lombardi

Players who question their playing time should first question their practice time.
Kevin Eastman

Everyone is born with a certain potential. You may never achieve your full potential, but how close you come depends on how much you want to pay the price.
Red Auerbach

Anytime you stop striving to get better, you're bound to get worse.
Pat Riley

Big things are accomplished only through the perfection of minor details.
John Wooden

You have to ask yourself, "Why am I not the best version of myself?"
John Calipari

If you don't do what's best for your body, you're the one who comes up on the short end.
Julius Erving

The pain, frustration and grinding, there's a toughness built in that process. When you come out the other side, you're much tougher.
Luke Walton

You must accept the fact that you have flaws and will need to work every day to become a better player than you were yesterday.
Dale Brown

Sometime in your life you will meet someone that will expect greatness from you.
Don Meyer

Don't succumb to excuses. Go back to the job of making the corrections and forming the habits that will make your goal possible.
Vince Lombardi

When you improve a little each day, eventually big things occur.
John Wooden

Don't try to be better than the other guy. Just try to be better than you were the day before. That's all you have to do.
Sam Wyche

Remember, Rome was not built in a day. Instant success is never possible. Competence results only from sustained, consistent, self-disciplined effort over an extended period of time.
Bud Wilkinson

Only to the extent that we expose ourselves over and over to annihilation can that which is indestructible be found in us.
Phil Jackson

Whether you know it or not, the habits you are developing now will be with you for the rest of your life.
John Wooden

To go from where you are to where you want to be — you have to have a dream, a goal, and you have to be willing to work for it.
Jim Valvano

Try not to do too many things at once. Know what you want, the number one thing today and tomorrow. Persevere and get it done.
George Allen

There is always someone better than you. Whatever it is that you do for a living, chances are, you will run into a situation in which you are not as talented as the person next to you. That's when being a competitor can make a difference in your fortunes.
Pat Summitt

It is not all about talent. It's about dependability, consistency, being coachable, and understanding what you need to do to improve.
Bill Belichick

Whatever muscles I have are the product of my own hard work and nothing else.
Evelyn Ashford

The five S's of sports training are stamina, speed, strength, skill, and spirit; but the greatest of these is spirit.
Ken Doherty

We get stronger when we test ourselves. Adversity can make us better. We must be challenged to improve, and adversity is the challenger.
John Wooden

Unless you try to do something beyond what you have already mastered, you will never grow. Every job is a self-portrait of the person who did it. Autograph your work with excellence.
Vince Lombardi

You must accept the fact that you have flaws and will need to work every day to become a better player than you were yesterday.
Dale Brown

Without self-discipline, success is impossible, period.
Lou Holtz

Racing is a matter of spirit not strength.
Janet Guthrie

I'm a runner because it taught me patience, endurance, and perseverance.
Cathy Freeman

Running alone is the toughest. You get to the point where you have to keep pushing yourself.
Walter Payton

There are no big things, only a logical accumulation of little things done at a very high standard of performance.
John Wooden

CHAPTER 8

Motivation

One of my favorite quotes on motivation comes from Zig Ziglar: *"People often say that motivation doesn't last. Well, neither does bathing. That's why we recommend it daily."*

His pithy saying on motivation is at the heart of why some people get motivated and others do not.

There are numerous sources of motivation for you to tap into, including family, friends, colleagues, and other coaches. You can find thousands of books, videos, and apps on how to get motivated. And while each will provide a different set of motivational stories and distinctive methodologies on how to get motivated, it all boils down to one key, fundamental point – your motivation is up to you.

Here's a tip for you: a heightened sense of self-satisfaction can be a valuable motivating factor. Knowing how pleased you will be with yourself once you have tackled or accomplished something is a sure-fire method to get you going, especially at the start of a task or during a long project when periods of lethargy and procrastination arise.

When it comes to motivating others, it is best to stay away from the "rah rah" and "you can do it, I know you can" type conversations. While these might work to help someone gain confidence and overcome an immediate struggle, they tend to have no lasting impact.

Motivating others can be quite challenging. For one thing, motivation is personal to each individual, as what motivates someone varies from person to person. Hence, you cannot motivate everyone on your team using the same methodology, techniques, or phrases.

Also, levels of motivation come and go, both collectively and individually. No one can stay highly motivated all the time, for doing so would likely result in burnout, fatigue, and an insensitivity to others. Plus, what motivates someone may alter over time or due to changing circumstances.

Additionally, workplace motivation is often impacted by non-workplace issues, situations, and circumstances (which are also constantly changing). Unfortunately, keeping people motivated is not easy.

As a leader and coach, you have to keep your finger on the "pulse" of your team members to ensure each is as motivated as possible at all times. At the same time, be leery of micro-managing your team members, for micromanagement tends to reduce employee motivation. On the other hand, autonomy and empowerment increase motivation, especially for confident staff, though doing so does come with increased risks.

Another key point, what motivates you may not motivate others on your team. For instance, if you find being publicly recognized by upper management or peers to be motivating, do not assume that everyone on your team feels the same way. Some may feel very uncomfortable or embarrassed with public praise and recognition. Giving them public accolades may be demotivating as they will want to avoid future feelings of embarrassment.

Here is my favorite quote from the words of wisdom in this section on motivation:

You can look for external sources of motivation
and that can catalyze a change,
but it won't sustain one.
It has to be from an internal desire.

Jillian Michaels

Quotes on Motivation

Confidence is contagious; so is lack of confidence.
Vince Lombardi

Believe deep down in your heart that you're destined to do great things.
Joe Paterno

If you are determined enough and willing to pay the price, you can get it done.
Mike Ditka

Ability is what you're capable of doing. Motivation determines what you do. Attitude determines how well you do it.
Lou Holtz

Despite the fear, finish the job.
Kobe Bryant

What makes you grind? You have to always be chasing something.
Ray Lewis

Don't think that you can make up for it by working twice as hard tomorrow. If you have it within your power to work twice as hard, why aren't you doing it now?
John Wooden

The ones who want to achieve and win championships motivate themselves.
Mike Ditka

In time, the people with desire will always rise to the top.
Bobby Unser

It's hard to beat a person that never gives up.
Babe Ruth

Make each day a masterpiece.
John Wooden

At the beginning of each new play, I thought of it as the most important play of the year. I went into it as if the game depended on it.
Merlin Olsen

Good, better, best. Never let it rest. Until your good is better and your better is best.
Tim Duncan

To succeed... you need to find something to hold on to, something to motivate you, something to inspire you.
Tony Dorsett

You can't put a limit on anything. The more you dream, the farther you get.
Michael Phelps

The most rewarding things you do in life are often the ones that look like they cannot be done.
Arnold Palmer

Learn to love the hate. Embrace it. Enjoy it. You earned it. Everyone is entitled to their own opinion and everyone should have one about you. Haters are a good problem to have. Nobody hates the good ones. They hate the great ones.
Kobe Bryant

If you aren't fired with enthusiasm, you will be fired with enthusiasm.
Vince Lombardi

The greatest opportunity in the world is found here today. We already know what yesterday has got for us. It's already gone. Tomorrow, too far away. What about right now!
Ray Lewis

Sometimes the biggest problem is in your head. You've got to believe.
Jack Nicklaus

There's always somebody saying you can't do it, and those people have to be ignored.
Bill Cartwright

You can do more. You can always do more.
Dan Marino

When anyone tells me I can't do anything, I'm just not listening any more.
Florence Griffith Joyner

Love never fails; character never quits. And with patience and persistence, dreams do come true.
Pete Maravich

It's the one thing you can control. You are responsible for how people remember you — or don't. So, don't take it lightly. If you do it right, your game will live on in others. You'll be imitated and emulated by those you played with, those you played against and those who never saw you play at all. So, leave everything on the court. Leave the game better than you found it. And when it comes time for you to leave, leave a legend.
Kobe Bryant

Do whatever you got to do to make sure you chase your legacy every second in your life.
Ray Lewis

If you don't have time to do it right, when will you have time to do it over?
John Wooden

Hard work beats talent when talent doesn't work hard.
Kevin Durant

The man who can drive himself further once the effort gets painful is the man who will win.
Roger Bannister

Don't look back. Something might be gaining on you.
Satchel Paige

I've always felt it was not up to anyone else to make me give my best.
Akeem Olajuwon

You can always become better.
Tiger Woods

I create my own path. It was straight and narrow. I looked at it this way: you were either in my way, or out of it. If you were standing between me and the game, I was going to knock you on your back and not feel bad about it. I was unapologetically me. That's all I ever wanted to be. I was never worried about my reputation — that's how I earned one. That's how I became the Black Mamba.
Kobe Bryant

As long as we persevere and endure, we can get anything we want.
Mike Tyson

I prepare so no one can take what is mine, no one can replace my mind, my heart.
Ray Lewis

I think the key is for women not to set any limits.
Martina Navratilova

Desire is the key to motivation, but it is determination and commitment to an unrelenting pursuit of your goal — a commitment to excellence — that will enable you to attain the success you seek.
Mario Andretti

Discipline yourself and others won't need to.
John Wooden

We get one opportunity in life, one chance at life to do whatever you're going to do, and lay your foundation and make whatever mark you're going to make. Whatever legacy you're going to leave; leave your legacy!
Ray Lewis

If you don't invest very much, then defeat doesn't hurt very much and winning is not very exciting.
Dick Vermeil

I don't think anything is unrealistic if you believe you can do it. I think if you are determined enough and willing to pay the price, you can get it done.
Mike Ditka

Everyone goes through adversity in life, but what matters is how you learn from it.
Lou Holtz

The biggest dreams aren't fueled by belief. They're fueled by doubt.
Kobe Bryant

The start is what stops most people.
Don Shula

Every morning in Africa a gazelle wakes up. It knows it must move faster than the lion or it will not survive. Every morning a lion wakes up and it knows it must move faster than the slowest gazelle or it will starve. It doesn't matter if you are the lion or the gazelle, when the sun comes up, you better be moving.
Roger Bannister

I am lucky that whatever fear I have within me, my desire to win is always stronger.
Serena Williams

Everything negative — pressures, challenges — is all an opportunity for me to rise.
Kobe Bryant

The difference between ordinary and extraordinary is that little extra.
Jimmy Johnson

Gray skies are just clouds passing over.
Frank Gifford

All your life you are told the things you cannot do. All your life they will say you're not good enough or strong enough; they will say you're the wrong height or the wrong weight or the wrong type to play this or be this or achieve this. They will tell you NO a thousand times, until all the no's become meaningless. All your life they will tell you no, quite firmly and very quickly. And you will TELL THEM YES.
Nike Ad

I learned that if you want to make it bad enough, no matter how bad it is, you can make it.
Gale Sayers

How old would you be if you didn't know how old you were?
Satchel Paige

This is the moment I accept the most challenging times will always be behind me AND in front of me.
Kobe Bryant

Love what you do. Believe in your instincts. And you'd better be able to pick yourself up and brush yourself off every day.
Mario Andretti

Will you be remembered, how would you be remembered, why wouldn't you fight for the greatest achievement ever?
Ray Lewis

If you aren't going all the way, why go at all?
Joe Namath

Pressure is playing for ten dollars when you don't have a dime in your pocket.
Lee Trevino

The battles that count aren't the ones for gold medals. The struggles within yourself — the invisible, inevitable battles inside all of us — that's where it's at.
Jesse Owens

I think anything is possible if you have the mindset and the will and desire to do it and put the time in.
Roger Clemens

I saw things differently. I didn't want to do what others had done. That didn't drive me, didn't get me in the gym before others got up. I wanted to do one better. Actually, I wanted to do a lot better. There were players I looked up to until I looked them square in the eyes. I know that one day, when I left the game, I didn't actually want to leave. I wanted to leave my mark.
Kobe Bryant

There's a spirit that grabs me, and it's in every one of you guys, but the question is, how much time are we wasting?
Ray Lewis

Being average means you are as close to the bottom as you are to the top.
John Wooden

One important key to success is self-confidence. An important key to self-confidence is preparation.
Arthur Ashe

Be willing to sacrifice anything, but compromise nothing in your quest to be your best.
Kobe Bryant

I don't focus on what I'm up against. I focus on my goals and I try to ignore the rest.
Venus Williams

If you don't have confidence, you'll always find a way not to win.
Carl Lewis

Just keep going. Everybody gets better if they keep at it.
Ted Williams

If there's something in your life that you know needs changing, make sure you change it before God's got to change it. Because if God's got to change it, you ain't going to like it.
Ray Lewis

You can look for external sources of motivation and that can catalyze a change, but it won't sustain one. It has to be from an internal desire.
Jillian Michaels

We all have self-doubt. You don't deny it, but you also don't capitulate to it. You embrace it.
Kobe Bryant

If the motivation is gone, then I am finished.
Marit Bjørgen

When you look at people who are successful, you will find that they aren't the people who are motivated, but have consistency in their motivation.
Arsène Wenger

Every day of my life I'm trying to find a different way to get better.
Ray Lewis

Once you know what failure feels like, determination chases success.
Kobe Bryant

Ability is a poor man's wealth.
John Wooden

You gotta be hungry for it. You've got to put everything you got on it. Everything! Every second. You have to be the first one in line. That's how leaders are born.
Ray Lewis

If you don't believe in yourself, no one will do it for you.
Kobe Bryant

Apathy can't be an excuse for inaction.
Bill Bradley

Optimism is a happiness magnet. If you stay positive, good things and good people will be drawn to you.
Mary Lou Retton

A positive attitude causes a chain reaction of positive thoughts, events, and outcomes. It is a catalyst, and it sparks extraordinary results.
Wade Boggs

Everything negative: pressure, challenges, is an opportunity for me to rise.
Kobe Bryant

Be a dreamer. If you don't know how to dream, you're dead.
Jim Valvano

Get comfortable with being uncomfortable!
Jillian Michaels

I figured something out. And it is no secret what I figured out. Whatever the majority of people were doing, I found myself doing the opposite. I wanted to chase something great.
Ray Lewis

The examples are endless but my philosophy is simple. Once I knew my seed, I was able to discover my muse and my purpose for being was crystal clear.
Kobe Bryant

Everybody wants to be somebody. The thing you have to do is give kids confidence they can. You have to give them a dream.
George Foreman

I like criticism. It makes you stronger.
LeBron James

If a coach can't trust your effort in the weight room, in the classroom, and at practice, how can you be trusted to play in a game?
Jeff Osterman

If you already know who you are, you may not become who you're supposed to be.
Mike Krzyzewski

Remember, your attitude toward a situation can help you to change it — you create the very atmosphere for defeat or victory.
Franco Harris

The day you think you can beat me, show me. Then move on to the next challenge.
Ray Lewis

It doesn't matter what your background is or where you come from, if you have dreams and goals, that's all that matters.
Serena Williams

Every day I go to work I compete for my job.
Larry Bird

If your why is strong enough you will figure out how!
Bill Walsh

Pride is a better motivator than fear.
John Wooden

The strength to make it becomes greater than the fear of missing it.
Kobe Bryant

Every boo on the road is a cheer.
Scotty Bowman

You don't always have to be THE best – just give people YOUR BEST.
Kevin Eastman

Either way, I refuse to change what I am. A lion has to eat. Run with me or run from me.
Kobe Bryant

Perform at your best when your best is required. Your best is required each day.
John Wooden

It's a daily decision to be uncommon.
Shaka Smart

No one has ever drowned in sweat.
Lou Holtz

Size doesn't make any difference; heart is what makes a difference.
Jerry Sloan

No one feels strong when she examines her own weaknesses. But in facing weakness, you learn how much there is in you, and you find real strength.
Pat Summitt

It is the brain, not the heart or lungs, that is the critical organ.
Roger Bannister

The last time I was intimidated was when I was 6 years old in karate class. I was an orange belt and the instructor ordered me to fight a black belt who was a couple years older and a lot bigger. I was scared s—less. I mean, I was terrified and he kicked my ass. But then I realized he didn't kick my ass as bad as I thought he was going to and that there was nothing really to be afraid of. That was around the time I realized that intimidation didn't really exist if you're in the right frame of mind.
Kobe Bryant

If tomorrow wasn't promised, what would you give for today?
Ray Lewis

Don't let what you cannot do interfere with what you can do.
John Wooden

CHAPTER 9

Bulletin Board Material

A nother way to motivate people is through pithy sayings and quotations. As a coach, you share these in a slide presentation, emails, wall posters, or handout cards.

I call these Bulletin Board Material. They are the kinds of motivational messages that sports coaches like to display in locker rooms and practice facilities.

The beauty of publicly displaying such motivational quotations is that your team members will see them frequently, helping to engrain the messages. They also serve as great reminders of your key development and motivational messages to your team members.

Here are 70 such messages for you to use with your players or team members.

Of these, my favorite amongst these words of wisdom in this section on bulletin board material is:

Dedication sees dreams come true.

Kobe Bryant

Bulletin Board Material Quotes

Always keep an open mind and a compassionate heart.
Phil Jackson

You can't let praise or criticism get to you. It's a weakness to get caught up in either one.
John Wooden

If you don't make a total commitment to whatever you're doing, then you start looking to bail out the first time the boat starts leaking.
Lou Holtz

Use misery to create mastery.
Kobe Bryant

The difference between the impossible and the possible lies in a man's determination.
Tommy Lasorda

The measure of who we are is what we do with what we have.
Vince Lombardi

Don't let anyone work harder than you do.
Serena Williams

It really doesn't cost anything to be nice, and the rewards can be unimaginable.
Paul (Bear) Bryant

The superior man blames himself. The inferior man blames others.
Don Shula

Don't waste talent. No matter what you do, don't waste talent.
Ray Lewis

Most people have the will to win, few have the will to prepare to win.
Bobby Knight

I can't believe that God put us on this earth to be ordinary.
Lou Holtz

One man practicing sportsmanship is far better than a hundred teaching it.
Knute Rockne

Never let the fear of striking out get in your way.
Babe Ruth

Gold medals aren't really made of gold. They're made of sweat, determination, and a hard-to-find alloy called guts.
Dan Gable

An athlete cannot run with money in his pockets. He must run with hope in his heart and dreams in his head.
Emil Zátopek

A winner never stops trying.
Tom Landry

To give anything less than your best is to sacrifice the gift.
Steve Prefontaine

It is better to look ahead and prepare than to look back and regret.
Jackie Joyner-Kersee

You can't let one bad moment spoil a bunch of good ones.
Dale Earnhardt

Success is one thing, impact is another.
Ray Lewis

Today I will do what others won't, so tomorrow I can accomplish what others can't.
Jerry Rice

Overpower. Overtake. Overcome.
Serena Williams

The winner ain't the one with the fastest car, it's the one who refuses to lose.
Dale Earnhardt

For everyone out there with a spark of genius, there are nine with ignition problems.
Julius Erving

Nothing will work unless you do.
John Wooden

The pain of discipline is far less than the pain of regret.
Sarah Bombell

The ideal attitude is to be physically loose and mentally tight.
Arthur Ashe

You were not born a winner, and you were not born a loser. You are what you make yourself be.
Lou Holtz

I think the real free person in society is one that is disciplined.
Dean Smith

Your mind is what makes everything else work.
Kareem Abdul-Jabbar

There has never been a great athlete who died not knowing what pain is.
Bill Bradley

Football doesn't build character. It eliminates weak ones.
Darrell Royal

Start where you are. Use what you have. Do what you can.
Arthur Ashe

Yesterday's home runs don't win today's games.
Babe Ruth

Never quit. Never give up.
Gabby Douglas

Dedication sees dreams come true.
Kobe Bryant

Every champion was once a contender that refused to give up.
Rocky Balboa

Most people fail, not because of lack of desire, but because of lack of commitment.
Vince Lombardi

What you are as a person is far more important than what you are as a basketball player.
John Wooden

The good Lord gave you a body that can stand most anything. It's your mind you have to convince.
Vincent Lombardi

Don't let yesterday take up too much of today.
John Wooden

The only way to defeat pain is to recognize pain exists.
Ray Lewis

Don't be a spectator, don't let life pass you by.
Lou Holtz

Humble enough to prepare, confident enough to perform.
Tom Coughlin

We don't live in our fears, we live in our hopes.
Mike Tomlin

I pray not for victory, but to do my best.
Amos Alonzo Stagg

The true athlete should have character, not be a character.
John Wooden

When the going gets tough, let the tough get going.
Frank Leahy

We don't quit, we don't cower, we don't run. We endure and conquer.
Kobe Bryant

If I don't get it right, I don't stop until I do.
Serena Williams

Excellence is not a skill. Excellence is an attitude.
Connor McGregor

Don't mistake activity with achievement.
John Wooden

Don't worry about losing. Think about winning.
Mike Krzyzewski

Body language never whispers. It SCREAMS!
Buzz Williams

I CAN'T = I Certainly Am Not Trying
Anonymous

Lack of effort bends me out of shape.
Bernadette Locke-Mattox

It's the little details that are vital. Little things make big things happen.
John Wooden

Never underestimate the heart of a champion.
Rudy Tomjanovich

It does not matter how many times you get knocked down, but how many times you get up.
Vince Lombardi

We're not going to be hanging around waiting for something to happen. We're going to make things happen ourselves.
Herb Brooks

It's only unthinkable if you don't think it.
Dabo Swinney

Everybody hears, but few listen.
Bobby Knight

The best players don't win games, the best teams do.
Tom Izzo

Things work out best for those who make the best of the way things work out.
John Wooden

Perfection is not attainable, but if we chase perfection, we can catch excellence.
Vince Lombardi

CHAPTER 10

Life Lessons

The world of sports is often a microcosm for life in general – full of ups, downs, setbacks, triumphs, disappointments, desires, hopes, and dreams.

It is said that the university of life provides our best lessons. I would agree with that, and add that the world of sports may be the second-best school for lessons applicable to life.

In the university of life, the lessons learned typically come from first-hand experiences. In the world of sports, we get to experience these lessons both as participants (first-hand) and as spectators (second-hand).

I believe one of the most important life lessons is summed up in one of my favorite sayings, *"Never stop learning, for life never stops teaching."*

I also believe that the best education comes not from being taught, but from being inspired. That's why one of my credos is, *"I would rather educate and inspire a hundred than teach a thousand."* Naturally, that is one of my motivators for creating this book of inspiration and motivational quotes – to help you on your life's journey and the many life lessons you will learn along the way.

Continuous learning is great, no matter the source. Whether the lessons come from the thrills of victories or the agony of defeats, we can all become better coaches, leaders, and humans by applying the lessons below to ourselves and our lives.

My favorite quote from the words of wisdom in this section on life lessons is:

*Make sure you're very courageous:
be strong, be extremely kind, and above all, be humble.*

Serena Williams

Quotes About Life Lessons

When things are going wrong, take a breath and reset yourself. You do that through mindfulness — you just come right back in and collect yourself.
Phil Jackson

It's not the load that breaks you down, it's the way you carry it.
Lou Holtz

The tennis ball doesn't know how old I am. The ball doesn't know if I'm a man or a woman or if I come from a communist country or not. Sport has always broken down these barriers.
Martina Navratilova

Young people need models, not critics.
John Wooden

Individuals with great self-esteem will do great things...they are the ones others count on to boost results when the company needs it most.
Rick Pitino

Trust me, setting things up right from the beginning will avoid a ton of tears and heartache.
Kobe Bryant

You're never as good as everyone tells you when you win, and you're never as bad as they say when you lose.
Lou Holtz

Make sure you're very courageous: be strong, be extremely kind, and above all be humble.
Serena Williams

Life is not a spectator sport. If you're going to spend your whole life in the grandstand just watching what goes on, in my opinion you're wasting your life.
Jackie Robinson

Never make excuses. Your friends don't need them and your foes won't believe them.
John Wooden

The lessons in my life have come from failures, my own shortcomings, naiveté, and buying into some of the biggest myths modern society has to sell.
Joe Gibbs

Difficulties in life are intended to make us better, not bitter.
Dan Reeves

No matter what accomplishments you make, somebody helped you.
Althea Gibson

Life is often compared to a marathon, but I think it is more like being a sprinter; long stretches of hard work punctuated by brief moments in which we are given the opportunity to perform at our best.
Michael Johnson

In a crisis, don't hide behind anything or anybody. They are going to find you anyway.
Paul (Bear) Bryant

Make the present good, and the past will take care of itself.
Knute Rockne

There's a choice that we have to make as people, as individuals. If you want to be great at something, there's a choice you have to make. We all can be masters at our craft, but you have to make a choice. What I mean by that is, there are inherent sacrifices that come along with that. Family time, hanging out with friends, being a great friend, being a great son, nephew, whatever the case may be. There are sacrifices that come along with making that decision.
Kobe Bryant

A bird doesn't sing because it has an answer, it sings because it has a song.
Lou Holtz

Adversity is the state in which man most easily becomes acquainted with himself, being especially free of admirers then.
John Wooden

Football is an honest game. It's true to life. It's a game about sharing. Football is a team game. So is life.
Joe Namath

Awards become corroded; friends gather no dust.
Jesse Owens

As you walk down the fairway of life you must smell the roses, for you only get to play one round.
Ben Hogan

It's hard for young players to see the big picture. They just see three or four years down the road.
Kareem Abdul-Jabbar

The worst thing about new books is that they keep us from reading the old ones.
John Wooden

You'll never get ahead of anyone as long as you try to get even with him.
Lou Holtz

It's the journey that matters. Learning is more important than the test. Practice well and the games will take care of themselves.
Tony Dungy

Never make a major decision based solely on money.
Chuck Noll

Nicklaus wanted to beat the man he was up against, not stomp his soul. In the 1959 U.S. Amateur final at The Broadmoor, Nicklaus and the great amateur Charlie Coe were locked in a sensational match. On one hole, Coe hit a beautiful chip next to the hole and scooped it up. Suddenly, it hit him: He hadn't putted out. Nicklaus, without looking up, said, "Don't worry about it, Charlie. That was good."
Rick Reilly

If you're not making mistakes, then you're not doing anything.
John Wooden

Loyalty and friendship, which is to me the same, created all the wealth that I've ever thought I'd have.
Ernie Banks

He (Cus D'Amato) taught me so many things, not just about boxing, which was a craft and could be mastered, but about living and about life, which is not so easily mastered.
Pete Hamill

Tell the truth. That way you don't have to remember a story.
John Wooden

When they walk away from the experience, I just want guys to say "I learned a lot about the game. I learned a lot about life through the game."
Bo Ryan

Some people are born on third base and go through life thinking they hit a triple.
Barry Switzer

Character is doing the right thing when nobody's looking. There are too many people who think that the only thing that's right is to get by, and the only thing that's wrong is to get caught.
J.C. Watts

A life isn't significant except for its impact on other lives.
Jackie Robinson

You can't live a perfect day without doing something for someone who will never be able to repay you.
John Wooden

Everything I saw, heard, read, or felt was viewed through the lens of growing as a basketball player. This perspective makes me curious about everything, makes everything interesting, and means that life is a living library where all I need to do is pay attention.
Kobe Bryant

If you build it they will come.
Field Of Dreams

Be more concerned with your character than your reputation, because your character is what you really are, while your reputation is merely what others think you are.
John Wooden

Work like you don't need the money, love like you've never been hurt, and dance like no one is watching.
Satchel Paige

I keep a lot of my opinions to myself.
Lee Trevino

Failure is not fatal, but failure to change might be.
John Wooden

Doing good feels better than doing bad. Believe me, I should know. I've gotten away with doing a lot of bad things. There's no satisfaction in that, only in doing good.
Mike Tyson

You can control your choice but once you make it, it controls you.
Bill Cowher

From what we get, we can make a living; what we give, however, makes a life.
Arthur Ashe

You must try to generate happiness within yourself. If you aren't happy in one place, chances are you won't be happy anyplace.
Ernie Banks

The true test of a man's character is what he does when no one is watching.
John Wooden

Our teachers, at the public-school level, are the most underpaid (for the importance of their job) in America.
Dean Smith

It doesn't bother me at all. Do I hold any hard feelings? Not at all. Life is too short to sit around and hold grudges. I don't hold any whatsoever.
Kobe Bryant

I don't think you're human if you don't get nervous.
Sidney Crosby

If you are caught on a golf course during a storm and are afraid of lightning, hold up a 1-iron. Not even God can hit a 1-iron.
Lee Trevino

Success is never final; failure is never fatal. It's courage that counts.
John Wooden

Show me someone who has done something worthwhile, and I'll show you someone who has overcome adversity.
Lou Holtz

As soon as you try to describe a close friendship, it loses something.
Dean Smith

The trouble in America is not that we are making too many mistakes, but that we are making too few.
Phil Knight

Sincerity may not help us make friends, but it will help us keep them.
John Wooden

Being able to touch so many people through my businesses, and make money while doing it, is a huge blessing.
Magic Johnson

My father gave me the greatest gift anyone could give another person: He believed in me.
Jim Valvano

The most important thing in the Olympic Games is not winning but taking part; the essential thing in life is not conquering but fighting well.
Pierre de Coubertin

All of life is peaks and valleys. Don't let the peaks get too high and the valleys too low.
John Wooden

Sports is such a great teacher. I think of everything they've taught me: camaraderie, humility, how to resolve differences.
Kobe Bryant

Talent is Nature-given. Be humble.
Fame is man-given. Be grateful.
Conceit is self-given. Be careful.
John Wooden

You have to be careful of people who like to talk a big game but can't back it up.
Ray Lewis

If you're bored with life, if you don't get up every morning with a burning desire to do things — you don't have enough goals.
Lou Holtz

Bravery is a complicated thing to describe. You can't say it's three feet long and two feet wide and that it weighs four hundred pounds or that it's colored bright blue or that it sounds like a piano or that it smells like roses. It's a quality, not a thing.
Mickey Mantle

The odd thing is that I wound up learning more about the world around me by having a singular focus inside of me.
Kobe Bryant

Forgiveness is that subtle thread that binds both love and friendship. Without forgiveness, you may not even have a child one day.
George Foreman

Be prepared and be honest.
John Wooden

You need to figure out a way to invest in the future of your family and friends. This sounds simple, and you may think it's a no-brainer, but take some time to think on it further. I said INVEST. I did not say GIVE.
Kobe Bryant

Accomplishment is something you cannot buy. If you have a chance and don't make the most of it, you are wasting your time on this earth.
Roberto Clemente

The quality of a person's life is in direct proportion to their commitment to excellence, regardless of their chosen field of endeavour.
Vince Lombardi

The first principle of contract negotiation is don't remind them of what you did in the past; tell them what you're going to do in the future.
Stan Musial

Bad things happen in life...but it's how you respond that counts.
Dabo Swinney

Realistic expectations for life are that we are going to be better today than we were yesterday, be better tomorrow than we were today. That's a plan for success.
Jim Harbaugh

Live by the creed that a strong work ethic, playing by the rules, and doing things the right way will bring about opportunities for success and, ultimately, happiness.
Nick Saban

In those moments when life's hard, be careful how you:
Speak to yourself.
Think of yourself.
Conduct yourself.
Develop yourself.
Tony Dungy

You don't get character because you're successful; you build character because of the hardships you face.
Herm Edwards

The value of being known as a person of character and integrity is priceless. It can't be bought. It's got to be earned.
Jim Harbaugh

If you smile, things will work out.
Serena Williams

There are many things that are essential to arriving at true peace of mind, and one of the most important is faith.
John Wooden

With all the things I've been through, the number one thing that I've learned is that we're supposed to help people through this world.
Ray Lewis

You win some and lose some in life. Some things are beyond your control. The main thing is to make choices for the right reason.
Dr. Jack Ramsay

Invest in great relationships, they will pay a lifetime of dividends.
Bill Walsh

Happiness begins where selfishness ends.
John Wooden

Experience is a hard teacher because she gives the test first, the lesson afterward.
Vernon Law

People who create 20% of the results will begin believing they deserve 80% of the rewards.
Pat Riley

You win in life with people, and that's important, because if you hang with winners, you stand a great chance of being a winner.
Pat Summitt

I don't think you should be guaranteed anything other than opportunity.
Lenny Wilkens

Good people are happy when something good happens to someone else.
Dean Smith

It takes a lot of energy to be negative. You have to work at it. But smiling is painless. I'd rather spend my energy smiling.
Eric Davis

The purpose of sport is to create better human beings. When you develop champions, you develop people who will change the world.
Mike Smith

Friendship is two-sided. It isn't a friend just because someone's doing something nice for you.
John Wooden

Adversity doesn't have to define you. Some of the worst things that happened to me in life, starting at a young age, some of the best things have followed.
Porter Moser

We should never discourage young people from dreaming dreams.
Lenny Wilkens

Crises are part of life. Everybody has to face them, and it doesn't make any difference what the crisis is.
Jack Nicklaus

When you face a crisis, you know who your true friends are.
Magic Johnson

There's more to life than basketball. The most important thing is your family and taking care of each other and loving each other no matter what.
Stephen Curry

I am going to spend my time today just thanking the people that played a role in my career, because I truly do believe that I was blessed by a lot of people that paths crossed mine as I went down the road in my career.
Nolan Ryan

You beat cancer by how you live, why you live, and the manner in which you live.
Stuart Scott

As cool as the other side of the pillow.
Stuart Scott

The older you get, the more goodbyes you say.
Mike Singletary

Every woman's success should be an inspiration to another. We're strongest when we cheer each other on.
Serena Williams

Life doesn't run away from nobody. Life runs at people.
Joe Frazier

CHAPTER 11

Yogisms

No book comprising quotations from the world of sports would be complete without a handful from the verbal master himself – Lawrence Peter "Yogi" Berra.

Berra played all but one of his 19 seasons in Major League Baseball for the New York Yankees. An 18-time All-Star, he played on 10 World Series championship teams, more than any other player in baseball history.

After his playing days, he managed both the Yankees, the New York Mets, and the Houston Astros. He is one of only seven managers to lead both American and National League teams to the World Series.

Known for his malapropisms, as well as a never-ending supply of unconventional witticisms and paradoxical statements, Berra was a reporter's delight.

I hope you enjoy this sample of what has become known as Yogi-isms.

Yogisms

Baseball is ninety percent mental and the other half is physical.
Yogi Berra

You got to be careful if you don't know where you're going, because you might not get there.
Yogi Berra

If you don't set goals, you can't regret not reaching them.
Yogi Berra

If you don't know where you are going, you'll end up someplace else.
Yogi Berra

You can observe a lot by just watching.
Yogi Berra

If the world were perfect, it wouldn't be.
Yogi Berra

I never said most of the things I said.
Yogi Berra

You can't think and hit at the same time.
Yogi Berra

It ain't over until it's over.
Yogi Berra

When you come to a fork in the road, take it.
Yogi Berra

It's like déjà vu all over again.
Yogi Berra

No one goes there nowadays, it's too crowded.
Yogi Berra

A nickel ain't worth a dime anymore.
Yogi Berra

Always go to other people's funerals, otherwise they won't come to yours.
Yogi Berra

We made too many wrong mistakes.
Yogi Berra

You wouldn't have won if we'd beaten you.
Yogi Berra

I usually take a two-hour nap from one to four.
Yogi Berra

Never answer an anonymous letter.
Yogi Berra

The future ain't what it used to be.
Yogi Berra

It gets late early out here.
Yogi Berra

Pair up in threes.
Yogi Berra

We have deep depth.
Yogi Berra

Why buy good luggage, you only use it when you travel.
Yogi Berra

I'm not going to buy my kids an encyclopedia. Let them walk to school like I did.
Yogi Berra

In theory, there is no difference between theory and practice. But, in practice, there is.
Yogi Berra

No one goes there nowadays, it's too crowded.
Yogi Berra

I always thought the record would stand until it was broken.
Yogi Berra

Love is the most important thing in the world, but baseball is pretty good, too.
Yogi Berra

Ninety percent of the game is half mental.
Yogi Berra

Take it with a grain of salt.
Yogi Berra

It was impossible to get a conversation going, everybody was talking too much.
Yogi Berra

You better cut the pizza in four pieces because I'm not hungry enough to eat six.
Yogi Berra

I want to thank you for making this day necessary.
Yogi Berra

If the people don't want to come out to the ballpark, nobody's going to stop them.
Yogi Berra

Slump? I ain't in no slump...I just ain't hitting.
Yogi Berra

We have deep depth.
Yogi Berra

I don't know (if they were men or women fans running naked across the field). They had bags over their heads.
Yogi Berra

I'm not going to buy my kids an encyclopedia. Let them walk to school like I did.
Yogi Berra

He hits from both sides of the plate. He's amphibious.
Yogi Berra

Even Napoleon had his Watergate.
Yogi Berra

If you ask me anything I don't know, I'm not going to answer.
Yogi Berra

Little League baseball is a very good thing because it keeps the parents off the streets.
Yogi Berra

Resources for Continued Leadership Development

The Art of Great Leadership online leadership education program

> https://theartofgreatleadership.com

Leadership Philosophy

> https://www.calienteleadership.com/the-importance-of-having-a-personal-leadership-philosophy/

Leadership Articles

> www.CalienteLeadership.com/Resources/leadership-articles

> https://www.linkedin.com/in/stevenbhoward/detail/recent-activity/posts/

Leadership Books

> www.CalienteLeadership.com/Resources/leadership-books

Steven Howard YouTube Channel

> https://www.youtube.com/channel/UCuZFGCoUe2jPRxqoeonhBnw

About the Author

Steven Howard is an award-winning author of 22 leadership, business, and motivational books. When he is not writing specializes in creating and delivering Leadership Development programs for frontline leaders, mid-level leaders, supervisors, senior leaders, and high-potential leaders.

He has trained and coached over 10,000 mid-level leaders, supervisors, managers, and senior leaders in Asia, Africa, Australia, Europe, Mexico, North America, and the

South Pacific. He has also coached youth baseball and basketball teams in Australia and the U.S.

Steven has over 40 years of international senior sales, marketing, and leadership experience. His corporate career covered a wide variety of fields and experiences, including Regional Marketing Director for Texas Instruments Asia-Pacific, Regional Director (South Asian & ASEAN) for TIME Magazine, Global Account Director at BBDO Advertising handling an international airline account, and Vice President Marketing for Citibank's Consumer Banking Group.

Since 1993 he has delivered leadership development programs in the U.S., Asia, Australia, Mexico, New Zealand, Fiji, Canada, Africa, Arabian Gulf, and Europe to numerous organizations, including Citicorp, Covidien, Danaher, DBS Bank, Deutsche Bank, DuPont Lycra, Esso Productions, ExxonMobil, Hewlett Packard, Imerys, Irving Oil, Micron Technology, Motorola Solutions, SapientNitro, Shire Pharmaceuticals, Standard Chartered Bank, and others.

He has been a member of the training faculty at MasterCard University Asia/Pacific, the Citibank Asia-Pacific Banking Institute, and Forum Corporation. He brings a truly international, cross-cultural perspective to his leadership development programs, having lived in Singapore for 21 years and in Australia for 12 years.

In addition to his leadership facilitation work, Steven has served on several Boards in both the private and non-profit sectors. He has also chaired a strategic advisory group for a local government entity and a national sporting organization that is a member of the Australian Olympic Committee.

Steven is the author of 22 leadership, marketing, and management books and the editor of nine professional and personal development books in the *Project You* series.

His other books are:

How Stress and Anxiety Impact Your Decision Making

Better Decisions Better Thinking Better Outcomes: How to go from Mind Full to Mindful Leadership

8 Keys to Becoming a Great Leader: With leadership lessons and tips from Gibbs, Yoda & Capt'n Jack Sparrow

Leadership Lessons from the Volkswagen Saga

Asian Words of Success

Indispensable Asian Words of Knowledge

Asian Words of Inspiration

Asian Words of Meaning

The Book of Asian Proverbs

Marketing Words of Wisdom

The Best of the Monday Morning Marketing Memo

Powerful Marketing Memos

Corporate Image Management: A Marketing Discipline

Powerful Marketing Minutes: 50 Ways to Develop Market Leadership

MORE Powerful Marketing Minutes: 50 New Ways to Develop Market Leadership

Asian Words of Wisdom

Asian Words of Knowledge

Essential Asian Words of Wisdom

Pillars of Growth: Strategies for Leading Sustainable Growth (co-author with three others)

Motivation Plus Marketing Equals Money (co-author with four others)

Contact Details

Email: steven@CalienteLeadership.com

Twitter: @stevenbhoward | @GreatLeadershp

LinkedIn: www.linkedin.com/in/stevenbhoward

Facebook: www.facebook.com/CalienteLeadership

Website: www.CalienteLeadership.com

Blog: CalienteLeadership.com/TheArtofGreatLeadershipBlog